MAKE YOUR CHURCH A HOLY GHOST CHURCH

"Follow after charity, and desire spiritual gifts"

GARY B. BAILEY

Holy Ghost Church Publishing

EPIGRAPH

"Make your church not only a Word church, but a Holy Ghost church.
Put the Word first always.
Move in the Holy Ghost in line with the Word.
And the glory shall be made manifest.
The glory shall even be seen by many.
And the blessings of the Lord will flow like a mighty river."

"Excerpt from a prophetic word delivered by Kenneth E. Hagin"
Winter Bible Seminar, February 18, 2003

COPYRIGHT

Published by Holy Ghost Church Publishing
An imprint of Reach The World Ministries
Dillsburg, Pennsylvania

For permissions and inquiries:
gbmin@mac.com

First Printing, May 2026
Printed in the United States of America
ISBN: 978-1-943256-04-4

Make Your Church a Holy Ghost Church

All Scripture quotations are taken from the King James Version of the Bible.

CONTENTS

PREFACE

~

In 1975, as a fifteen-year-old freshman in high school, I was filled with the Holy Ghost and spoke with other tongues. It was a life-changing moment for me.

I had been raised in a church that taught me the Scriptures from the pulpit and in Sunday school, and I remain deeply grateful for that foundation. It was a nurturing environment, and many truths were planted in my heart as a young person. But when I was filled with the Holy Ghost, the Bible began to open to me in a new way. I began to see the Scriptures not only as historic truth, but as truth that could be believed, received, and practiced in the present day.

In the years that followed, I was introduced to charismatic and full gospel circles. I listened to Christian radio preachers and teachers, read the literature I could find, and visited Christian bookstores regularly. The charismatic renewal was in full swing, and many young people in our church youth group were also filled with the Holy Ghost during those years. God was moving, and I was hungry to understand what He was doing.

As a young believer, I began to see the benefit of speaking with tongues in my own devotional life. I learned that praying in the Spirit brought personal edification and spiritual strength. Early on, I sensed the call of God upon my life, and after graduating from high school I attended Bible school at Rhema Bible Training Center in Oklahoma. That season of training helped set the course for my life and ministry.

Through the years, I have served in helps ministry, pastored churches, and traveled as an itinerant minister. During that time, I discovered that many sincere believers and many good churches had very little practical understanding concerning the Holy Ghost, the gifts of the Spirit, and the operation of spiritual utterance in the local church.

In 2005, I was introduced to Evangelist Joe Jordan, who later introduced me to the ministry and influence of J. R. Goodwin and First Assembly of God in Pasadena, Texas. Joe had served as song leader for Mom and Dad Goodwin in the early 1960s. I spent many hours speaking with him in person and by phone about the move of the Spirit in the local church. Much of the teaching in this book has its roots in those conversations.

I mention the Goodwins because Dad Goodwin understood the move of the Spirit in the local church in a remarkable way. In the mid-1960s, Howard Carter, an early Pentecostal pioneer, visited their church in his later years. After observing the services, he said it was the greatest move of the Spirit, with the greatest order, that he had seen anywhere in the world.

From 2009 until approximately April 2013, I participated in a Bible forum in Kansas City conducted by Dr. Ron Smith and Joe Jordan. In the 1960s, Dr. Smith had served as associate pastor at Dad Goodwin's church for eight years.

On one occasion, before that day's forum began, I asked both Dr. Ron and Joe Jordan whether they could remember a regular service at the Goodwins' church where tongues and interpretation did not occur. They looked at one another, thought for a moment, and both said they did not remember such a time.

That testimony stayed with me.

This book is written to ask whether our churches have settled for less than the New Testament pattern. A careful study of Scripture answers that question and shows us the remedy. The answer is not to invent something new, chase spiritual novelty, or abandon order. The answer is to return to what the Word of God permits, provides, and governs. Paul spoke of a gathered church where there may be a psalm, a doctrine, a tongue, a revelation, and an interpretation, and then he gave the governing rule: "Let all things be done unto edifying" (1 Corinthians 14:26).

I believe tongues, interpretation of tongues, prophecy, and other manifestations of the Spirit are meant to function in the local church with consistency, reverence, order, and love. I encourage you to read thoughtfully and prayerfully, and to consider what we may be missing in our worship services when we make little room for the Holy Ghost.

The Author

~

We have a say in the kind of church in which we are involved. The spiritual character of a congregation is shaped by what is taught, what is believed, what is expected, what is welcomed, and what leaders and believers make room for.

Jesus said, "I will build my church; and the gates of hell shall not prevail against it" (Matthew 16:18). Ultimately, Jesus is the builder, author, and foundation of every true church. No man can build the Church apart from Him, and no church can become what God intended by human effort alone.

Yet Jesus works through people. He raises up leaders. He gathers believers of like precious faith. He strengthens willing hands for the work of His house. The Lord said through the prophet Zechariah, "Let your hands be strong" (Zechariah 8:9). God's people have always had a part to play in carrying out His work in the earth.

On February 18, 2003, Kenneth E. Hagin gave a prophetic admonition that has stayed with me for years: "Make your church not only a Word church, but a Holy Ghost church." That sentence is the seed thought behind this book.

To make your church a Holy Ghost church is not to build something apart from Christ. It is to cooperate with what Jesus desires for His Church. It is to honor the Word, welcome the Spirit, and make room for the present ministry of the Holy Ghost among the people of God.

The Word must always come first. The Word is our foundation, our safeguard, and our final authority. The Church can honor the Word fully while also giving room to the Holy Spirit who inspired it. We do not have to choose between sound doctrine and spiritual life, between Scripture and the present ministry of the Holy Ghost. We need the Word, and we need the Holy Ghost.

In recent years, many believers have quietly questioned the necessity of gathering when sermons, podcasts, and live streams are available at any moment. These tools may serve a helpful purpose, but they can never replace what happens when God's people assemble and the Holy Spirit is given liberty to move. A church that consistently makes room for the operation of the Spirit offers more than church as usual. It provides an encounter with the manifest presence of God.

This book is written for pastors, leaders, and hungry believers who desire a genuine move of the Spirit in their midst. It is a call to return to the New Testament pattern: the Word honored, the Spirit welcomed, Jesus glorified, and the people of God edified.

Where the Word is honored and the Spirit is welcomed, believers are strengthened, the Church is built up, and the reality of God's presence is unmistakable.

~

PART I
DON'T BE IGNORANT

"Now concerning spiritual gifts, brethren, I would not have you ignorant."
— 1 Corinthians 12:1

CHAPTER 1

WHAT IS A HOLY GHOST CHURCH?

A Holy Ghost church is defined by the presence and work of the Holy Spirit.

It is more than a church with good music, good preaching, a friendly atmosphere, and well-organized programs. Those things have value, but they are no substitute for what God intended to be present and active in the assembly. Programs may help a church function, but only the Spirit of God gives it life.

From the beginning, God did not intend His people to operate in human strength alone. Jesus said, “without me ye can do nothing” (John 15:5). The Church was never meant to depend merely on talent, structure, personality, or organization. Those things may serve a purpose, but they can never replace the power and presence of the Holy Ghost.

Before Jesus ascended, He gave His disciples a command:

“And, behold, I send the promise of my Father upon you: but tarry ye in the city of Jerusalem, until ye be endued with power from on high.”

— Luke 24:49

These were men who had walked with Jesus, heard His teaching, seen His miracles, and witnessed His resurrection. Yet He still told them not to go forward until they received power from on high.

That tells us something important: The Church was never meant to function without that power.

THE CHURCH NEEDS THE ANOINTING

Jesus Himself said, "The Spirit of the Lord is upon me, because he hath anointed me to preach the gospel to the poor..." (Luke 4:18). If the Son of God ministered under the anointing of the Spirit, the Church should not think it can fulfill its calling by information, organization, or religious form alone.

The anointing is not human ability or religious excitement. It is the Spirit of God upon a person because God has given him a work to do. Jesus was anointed to preach, heal, deliver, and set at liberty. The anointing is never without purpose. In the same way, the Church needs the anointing of the Holy Ghost because there is still a work to do, a Gospel to preach, people to help, and a world to reach.

A Holy Ghost church, therefore, is a church where the Word is honored, the Spirit is welcomed, and the presence of God is recognized in a tangible way. It is New Testament Christianity: Word and Spirit together.

THE CHURCH IS SHAPED BY WHAT IT WELCOMES

The kind of church we have is not accidental. Churches are shaped over time by what is taught, what is expected, what is permitted, what is resisted, and what is given room to operate.

If a church makes room only for preaching, singing, announcements, and programs, then those things will define the life of the church. But if a church teaches the Word, welcomes the Spirit, and makes room for the Holy Ghost to move, then the congregation begins to develop a different expectation.

What is welcomed becomes normal.

What is ignored becomes rare.

What is taught becomes understood.

What is practiced becomes part of the spiritual life of the people.

This is why a Holy Ghost church must be intentional. A church does not drift into the move of the Spirit. It must be taught, led, and shepherded in that direction.

This does not mean man controls the Holy Ghost. No pastor can manufacture the gifts of the Spirit. No congregation can force God to move. But leaders and believers can obey Scripture. They can desire spiritual gifts. They can make room. They can remove unnecessary fear. They can learn the order of the Word. They can yield when the Spirit prompts.

God supplies the power, but His people must cooperate with Him.

LEADERSHIP AND THE SPIRITUAL CLIMATE

Leadership helps shape the spiritual climate of a church.

Throughout Scripture, when God wanted to do something among His people, He often raised up a leader. God uses people who will yield to Him.

The Lord said to Moses:

“Come now therefore, and I will send thee unto Pharaoh,

that thou mayest bring forth my people the children of Israel out of Egypt."

— Exodus 3:10

After Moses, the Lord spoke to Joshua:

"Moses my servant is dead; now therefore arise, go over this Jordan, thou, and all this people."

— Joshua 1:2

In the days of the judges, Scripture says:

"Nevertheless the LORD raised up judges, which delivered them out of the hand of those that spoiled them."

— Judges 2:16

God also prepared David to rule in Israel. The Bible says:

"He chose David also his servant, and took him from the sheepfolds."

— Psalm 78:70

Again and again in Scripture, God raises up leaders to fulfill His purposes.

Scripture also shows that leaders and people influence one another spiritually. Through Hosea, the Lord said:

"And there shall be, like people, like priest: and I will punish them for their ways, and reward them their doings."

— Hosea 4:9

In its setting, this is a word of judgment to a people and priesthood that had departed from the knowledge of God. But the principle remains clear: leadership matters. The spiritual condition of the leaders affects the spiritual condition of the people. What is honored in the pulpit will usually be honored in the congregation. What is neglected in leadership will often be neglected among the people.

This is one reason the subject of the Holy Ghost must not be ignored. If leaders neglect the Word concerning the working of the Holy Spirit, the people will often remain uninstructed. If leaders are silent about the manifestations of the Spirit, the congregation may become unfamiliar with what God has plainly placed in the Church.

A church is shaped by what is taught, what is desired, and what is given room to operate. When leaders preach the promises of God and teach what Scripture makes available, hunger can rise in the hearts of the people.

This is why leadership matters. A church does not change by accident. It must be taught, modeled, and led.

This matters in the local church. A church is not shaped by leadership alone, but leadership carries real responsibility. Leaders help establish direction, boundaries, expectation, and spiritual culture. A pastor is not the Holy Spirit, but he is responsible to help create an atmosphere where the Holy Spirit is welcomed and obeyed.

In the New Testament, Jesus gave ministry gifts to the Church:

"And he gave some, apostles; and some, prophets; and some, evangelists; and some, pastors and teachers."

— Ephesians 4:11

God gives leaders because leadership matters. He gives ministry gifts "for the perfecting of the saints, for the work of the ministry, for the edifying of the body of Christ."

— Ephesians 4:12

Leaders are not given to replace the body. They are given to equip the body. A healthy church is not built by one person doing everything while everyone else watches. It is built when leaders equip, believers grow, and the whole body learns to function under the headship of Christ.

THE PEOPLE ALSO HAVE A PART

A Holy Ghost church is not made by leadership only. The congregation also has a part to play.

Believers help create a spiritual atmosphere through hunger, faith, expectancy, obedience, and yieldedness.

A pastor may teach on the Holy Spirit, but the people must receive the Word. A pastor may make room for the Spirit, but the congregation must learn to respond. A pastor may encourage spiritual gifts, but believers must desire them and yield to the Spirit in love and order.

Paul wrote:

"Follow after charity, and desire spiritual gifts."

— 1 Corinthians 14:1

That instruction was not written to leaders only. It was written to the entire church. The whole congregation has a responsibility to walk in love and desire the things of the Spirit.

A church becomes strong when leaders and believers are moving in the same direction. Leaders teach and shepherd. Believers yield, pray, and participate. Together, they make room for the Holy Ghost to minister according to the Word.

This is not human effort replacing divine power. It is believers cooperating with divine power.

THE CHURCH BELONGS TO CHRIST

The Church does not belong to man. It belongs to Jesus Christ.

When Jesus asked His disciples, "But whom say ye that I am?" Peter answered:

"Thou art the Christ, the Son of the living God."

— Matthew 16:16

Jesus replied:

"Blessed art thou, Simon Barjona: for flesh and blood hath not revealed it unto thee, but my Father which is in heaven.

And I say also unto thee, That thou art Peter, and upon this rock I will build my church; and the gates of hell shall not prevail against it."

— Matthew 16:17–18

Peter did not receive this by flesh and blood. It was revealed to him by the Father. He saw by revelation that Jesus was not merely a prophet, teacher, or miracle worker. He was the Christ, the Son of the living God.

When Jesus said, "upon this rock I will build my church," He was speaking of the rock of revelation: Jesus Christ unveiled to the heart of man by the Father. Peter received revealed knowledge of who Jesus was. The Church is not built upon Peter as a man, human personality, natural ability, or religious organization. The Church is built upon the revelation of Jesus Christ.

The Church is founded upon the revelation of Christ, and it matures as Christ continues to be made known through the Word and by the Spirit. True revelation agrees with Scripture and makes Christ known more clearly — who He is, what He has done, what He is doing, and what He has given to His people.

True revelation will always keep Jesus Christ at the center. The angel said to John:

"And I fell at his feet to worship him. And he said unto me, See thou do it not: I am thy fellowservant, and of thy brethren that have the testimony of Jesus: worship God: for the testimony of Jesus is the spirit of prophecy."

— Revelation 19:10

That statement is important. The spirit of prophecy is not the exaltation of man. It is not spiritual display. It is the testimony of Jesus. Genuine prophecy and true revelation do not draw attention away from Christ. They reveal Him, honor Him, agree with His Word, and bear witness to who He is.

This helps us understand why revelation matters in the Church. The Church is built upon the revelation of Jesus Christ, and every true operation of the Spirit will be consistent with that foundation.

Jesus said, "I will build my church." That statement keeps everything in its proper place. The Church is His. He is the builder. He is the head. The Church belongs to Him. At the same time, He works through people who are surrendered to His will. He gives ministry gifts. He equips the saints. He strengthens His people for the work He has called them to do.

But no man owns the Church. No pastor owns the Church. No congregation owns the Church. The Church belongs to Jesus Christ.

A Holy Ghost church is not a church trying to build something apart from Christ. It is a church cooperating with the One who said, "I will build my church."

Leaders teach. Believers respond. The Word is honored. The Spirit is welcomed. Prayer, worship, the gifts of the Spirit, and the correction and order of Scripture are given room to operate.

When leaders and believers yield to God and make room for the Holy Ghost, the Church is strengthened according to Christ's own design.

WORD AND SPIRIT TOGETHER

A Holy Ghost church does not despise structure, planning, or preparation. These things can serve the purposes of God, but they must never become a substitute for the life of the Spirit. Planning and preparation should serve the move of God, not replace it.

The Word gives us the foundation.

The Spirit gives life and power.

The Word gives boundaries.

The Spirit moves within those boundaries.

The Word keeps us from error.

The Spirit keeps us from dead formality.

A church should never have to choose between the Word and the Spirit. We need both. The New Testament pattern is not Word without Spirit or Spirit without Word. It is the Word honored and the Spirit welcomed.

When the Word and Spirit work together, believers are edified, the Church is strengthened, and even an unbeliever may sense that something supernatural is happening among God's people.

That is a Holy Ghost church.

CHAPTER 2

QUALITIES OF A HOLY GHOST CHURCH

A Holy Ghost church believes in the baptism with the Holy Ghost. It presents this promise clearly and helps hungry hearts receive the precious infilling of the Holy Spirit.

Jesus said:

"But ye shall receive power, after that the Holy Ghost is come upon you: and ye shall be witnesses unto me both in Jerusalem, and in all Judaea, and in Samaria, and unto the uttermost part of the earth."

— Acts 1:8

But a Holy Ghost church is not marked by doctrine alone. It is also marked by faith, love, courage, waiting, and yieldedness. These qualities help remove unnecessary barriers so the Spirit of God may minister freely among His people.

Some believers have concluded that the safest posture is distance. They have seen confusion or extremes and backed away from the manifestations of the Spirit altogether. But the answer to misuse is not disuse. When the gifts of the Spirit have been handled wrongly, the answer is not to throw them away, but to return to Scripture and learn how they are to operate in a right and orderly way. Obedience to Scripture is key. A Holy Ghost church is a place where people do not fear the gifts of the Spirit or abuse them. They learn what Scripture says, and they follow it.

A CHURCH OF FAITH

A Holy Ghost church is a church of faith. Faith responds to what God has said. A church of faith does not merely agree with Scripture. It acts on it.

One major thing that distinguishes a church is whether it is willing to be a doer of the Word and not a hearer only. Many churches have good doctrine on paper, but that doctrine is never carried over into actual practice in the church. That is a serious problem. It is possible to believe the right things in theory while failing to obey them in practice.

James wrote:

"But be ye doers of the word, and not hearers only, deceiving your own selves."

—James 1:22

A Holy Ghost church must not only believe what the Bible says about the Holy Ghost, spiritual gifts, prayer, worship, and the gathered assembly. It must act on what the Bible says. Faith does not simply admire truth. Faith obeys truth.

If the Bible says, "Covet earnestly the best gifts" (1 Corinthians 12:31), then faith says, "Lord, we desire what You desire for the Church." If the Bible says, "Follow after charity, and desire spiritual gifts" (1 Corinthians 14:1), then faith says, "We will not draw back from what God has made available to the Church."

Faith acts. Faith makes room for God to speak, move, and manifest Himself in ways that help His people.

A CHURCH THAT WALKS IN LOVE

A Holy Ghost church is a church that walks in love.

Love is the motive behind every genuine work of the Spirit. The gifts of the Spirit are not given for display, competition, or personal recognition. They are given to help people and edify the Church.

This is why Paul placed 1 Corinthians 13 between 1 Corinthians 12 and 1 Corinthians 14. In chapter 12, he teaches concerning the manifestations of the Spirit. In chapter 14, he gives instruction concerning tongues, interpretation, prophecy, edification, and order in the gathered assembly. But between those two chapters, Paul speaks of love.

"Though I speak with the tongues of men and of angels, and have not charity, I am become as sounding brass, or a tinkling cymbal."

— 1 Corinthians 13:1

Paul was not setting love against the gifts of the Spirit. He was showing the proper motive and atmosphere in which the gifts are to operate. The gifts are real and necessary, but without love they do not accomplish what God intended.

Paul had already said:

"But covet earnestly the best gifts: and yet shew I unto you a more excellent way."

— 1 Corinthians 12:31

The more excellent way is love. Love does not replace the gifts, but it governs their operation. Love keeps the gifts from becoming harsh, prideful, self-centered, or disorderly.

If our motivation is love, we will want the gifts to operate because they bless and strengthen the Church. A word of prophecy can edify, exhort, and comfort. A word of wisdom can bring direction. A word of knowledge can uncover what is hidden. A gift of faith can bring courage to obey God. These gifts are not toys. They are tools of love.

A Holy Ghost church should desire spiritual gifts, but it must desire them in the spirit of love. It should make room for manifestation, but always for the purpose of edification.

A Holy Ghost church is not only a church where the gifts of the Spirit are welcomed. It is a church where the love of God governs everything those gifts are meant to do.

A CHURCH THAT IS COURAGEOUS

A Holy Ghost church is a courageous church.

Paul wrote to Timothy:

"For God hath not given us the spirit of fear; but of power, and of love, and of a sound mind."

— 2 Timothy 1:7

Believers may be hesitant, not because they are resisting God, but because they simply do not recognize the move of the Spirit or know how to respond to Him.

They may not know how to process what they sense, or how to yield without stirring unnecessary confusion or tension.

This is why careful teaching and wise pastoral leadership matter. When a church is taught the Word and pastored with wisdom, fear begins to loosen its grip. People begin to understand that God can use ordinary believers when they are willing to yield to the Holy Ghost.

A Holy Ghost church is not reckless, but neither is it ruled by fear. It walks in power, love, and a sound mind.

A CHURCH THAT WAITS UPON THE LORD

A Holy Ghost church learns to wait upon the Lord.

Isaiah wrote:

"But they that wait upon the LORD shall renew their strength;

they shall mount up with wings as eagles;

they shall run, and not be weary;

and they shall walk, and not faint."

— Isaiah 40:31

Waiting does not have to be long to be meaningful. Even a brief moment of expectancy can lift the level of faith in a room. People stop rushing. Hearts become still. Ears become open. Believers begin to listen.

A church service can make room for this without becoming awkward. If leadership prepares the church, people understand, "This is a moment to wait upon the Lord." It may be a few minutes, or it may be longer at times.

That quality of waiting raises expectancy for the Spirit of God to move, whether through tongues, interpretation, prophecy, or another manifestation of the Spirit. A church that waits upon the Lord is not wasting time. It is making room for God.

A CHURCH THAT YIELDS

A Holy Ghost church is a church that yields.

Paul wrote:

"Neither yield ye your members as instruments of unrighteousness unto sin: but yield yourselves unto God, as those that are alive from the dead, and your members as instruments of righteousness unto God."

— Romans 6:13

Yieldedness begins with presenting ourselves to God. None of the gifts operate without yieldedness. People cannot speak out by faith if they refuse to yield. A tongue, an interpretation, or a prophecy is a Spirit-inspired utterance, but it still requires a believer's cooperation.

The Spirit does not force people. He leads. He prompts. He gives utterance, and believers respond.

These qualities create strength and stability because the same Spirit who empowers the Church also produces spiritual fruit and godly character. A Holy Ghost church is not only open to the power of the Spirit; it is also shaped by the character of the Spirit.

Before we can understand the gifts of the Spirit in public worship, we must first understand the work of the Holy Spirit in the individual believer. These qualities prepare the church to receive what God has promised and to handle spiritual things with faith, love, and order.

CHAPTER 3

THE HOLY SPIRIT IN THE LIFE OF THE BELIEVER

Before we speak about the gifts of the Spirit in the local church, we must understand the Holy Spirit's work in the believer. Many sincere Christians are confused here. Some assume that being saved is the same as being filled with the Holy Ghost. They assume they have received everything the New Testament offers simply by accepting Jesus Christ as Lord and Savior.

Salvation is a miracle. It is the new birth. It is essential. But Scripture also speaks of the baptism with the Holy Ghost as a distinct experience, and that distinction must be made clear.

BAPTIZED INTO THE BODY

At salvation, the Holy Spirit brings us into Christ.

"For by one Spirit are we all baptized into one body..."

— 1 Corinthians 12:13

The word "baptized" carries the idea of being placed into, immersed, or brought fully into something. Scripture speaks of baptism in more than one way. In water baptism, the believer is immersed in water as an outward testimony of his identification with Christ. Here, Paul is speaking of what happens when a person is saved: the Spirit of God places us into the body of Christ.

We are brought into Christ. We are made part of His body. We are brought into the family of God. We become new creatures in Christ.

At this point, a person is born of the Spirit, and the Holy Spirit indwells the believer. This is the life within.

A SIMPLE DISTINCTION

It may help to see the distinction clearly.

The Holy Spirit baptizes the believer into the body of Christ, while Jesus baptizes the believer with the Holy Ghost.

One brings us into Christ. This is necessary for salvation.

The other clothes us with power to be witnesses and to live the Christian life.

John the Baptist pointed forward to the baptism with the Holy Ghost when he said of Jesus:

"He shall baptize you with the Holy Ghost, and with fire."

— Matthew 3:11

This does not lessen salvation. It does not replace salvation. It does not compete with salvation. It is another promise for the believer, an empowerment from on high.

A PERSONAL MOMENT

As a young person, I was hungry for God and set myself to seek the Lord as best I could. At that time in my life, I had been born again for several years. During my freshman year of high school, two or three times a week, I sat alone at a library cubicle and prayed a simple prayer: "Lord, use my life." At the time, I was ignorant of the baptism with the Holy Ghost as the New Testament describes it.

In May of 1975, a friend visited our home and showed me from the Scriptures the baptism with the Holy Ghost. The church I attended taught the Bible, but never spoke of this particular doctrine. After sharing with me from the Bible, my friend laid hands on me, and I was filled with the Spirit and began to speak with other tongues.

I had received the Holy Spirit, but I still did not fully understand the Scriptures concerning this baptism. After a year or so, I heard a pastor teach along these lines and obtained material that clearly taught the subject. During that first year, I did not fully comprehend what I had experienced.

One thing was certain: my life had changed, and God had met me.

"HAVE YE RECEIVED?"

The book of Acts makes the distinction plain. In Acts 19, Paul met believers and asked:

"Have ye received the Holy Ghost since ye believed?"

— Acts 19:2

Paul would not have asked that question if the baptism with the Holy Ghost occurred automatically at salvation. He asked because it is distinct from the new birth. Scripture presents it as a normal and expected experience for believers.

LIFE WITHIN AND POWER UPON

The Spirit within gives life.

The Spirit upon gives power.

The Spirit within bears witness that we belong to God.

The Spirit upon empowers us to be witnesses.

This is why the baptism with the Holy Ghost matters. God never intended for the Church to rely on human strength alone. He provides help. He provides power. He provides the Spirit.

Understanding this prepares us for what comes next: tongues as the initial evidence and the operation of the gifts in the local church.

CHAPTER 4

TONGUES: THE INITIAL EVIDENCE

When the Holy Spirit was poured out on the Day of Pentecost, Scripture tells us plainly what happened:

"And they were all filled with the Holy Ghost, and began to speak with other tongues, as the Spirit gave them utterance."

— Acts 2:4

They were filled.

The Spirit gave the utterance.

And they spoke.

God did not leave the early believers wondering whether His promise had come to pass. It was clear and recognizable.

NOT AN ISOLATED MOMENT

If Acts 2:4 were the only passage of Scripture describing believers receiving the Holy Ghost, some might assume it was a singular event on the Day of Pentecost. But the baptism with the Holy Ghost does not stand alone. The New Testament reveals a consistent pattern: those who believed on Jesus were filled with the Holy Ghost, and speaking with tongues is repeatedly connected with that experience.

The book of Acts records several instances where people believed the gospel and then received the Holy Ghost in a definite and recognizable way.

ACTS 8: THE SAMARITANS RECEIVED

In Acts 8, Philip went down to Samaria and preached Christ. The people received the Word with joy and believed the gospel.

"Then Philip went down to the city of Samaria, and preached Christ unto them."

— Acts 8:5

"And there was great joy in that city."

— Acts 8:8

"But when they believed Philip preaching the things concerning the kingdom of God, and the name of Jesus Christ, they were baptized, both men and women."

— Acts 8:12

These people had believed the gospel and had been baptized. They were not unbelievers. Yet when the apostles at Jerusalem heard that Samaria had received the Word of God, they sent Peter and John to them.

"Now when the apostles which were at Jerusalem heard that Samaria had received the word of God, they sent unto them Peter and John:

Who, when they were come down, prayed for them, that they might receive the Holy Ghost:

(For as yet he was fallen upon none of them: only they were baptized in the name of the Lord Jesus.)

Then laid they their hands on them, and they received the Holy Ghost."

— Acts 8:14–17

This shows that believers can truly be saved and yet still need to receive the promise of the Spirit of which Jesus spoke. The believers in Samaria were first born of the Spirit and later filled with the Spirit.

Acts 8 does not specifically say they spoke with tongues, but something visible and recognizable happened when they received the Holy Ghost.

"And when Simon saw that through laying on of the apostles' hands the Holy Ghost was given, he offered them money."

— Acts 8:18

Simon saw that something had happened. The passage shows clearly that receiving the Holy Ghost was a definite experience after they had believed.

ACTS 9: SAUL OF TARSUS RECEIVED

In Acts 9, Saul of Tarsus met the Lord on the road to Damascus. The Lord then sent Ananias to him, and Scripture says:

"And Ananias went his way, and entered into the house; and putting his hands on him said, Brother Saul, the Lord, even Jesus, that appeared unto thee in the way as thou camest, hath sent me, that thou mightest receive thy sight, and be filled with the Holy Ghost."

— Acts 9:17

Saul had already encountered Jesus as Lord, yet Ananias was sent to lay hands on him so that he might receive his sight and be filled with the Holy Ghost. This shows that receiving the Holy Ghost was not limited to the original disciples at Pentecost. Even the man who had persecuted the Church was brought into the fullness of this New Testament experience.

Acts 9 does not specifically say that Paul spoke with tongues at that moment, but Paul later wrote:

"I thank my God, I speak with tongues more than ye all."

— 1 Corinthians 14:18

This shows that tongues were part of Paul's own Spirit-filled life.

ACTS 10: THE GENTILES RECEIVED

In Acts 10, the promise reached beyond the Jewish people and the Samaritans. While Peter preached in Cornelius' house, the Holy Ghost fell on those who heard the Word.

Peter and those who came with him knew the Spirit had been poured out because they heard them speak with tongues.

"For they heard them speak with tongues, and magnify God."

— Acts 10:46

They heard them speak with tongues. This was the sign that convinced the Jewish believers that the Gentiles had received the same gift. The promise was not for Israel only. It was for all who would believe.

ACTS 19: THE DISCIPLES AT EPHESUS RECEIVED

In Acts 19, Paul met certain disciples at Ephesus and asked them a direct question:

"Have ye received the Holy Ghost since ye believed?"

— Acts 19:2

That question would make no sense if receiving the Holy

Ghost were automatic in every sense at the moment a person believed. Paul recognized that people could be disciples and still need to receive the Holy Ghost in this fuller New Testament sense.

After Paul instructed them and laid hands on them, Scripture says:

"And when Paul had laid his hands upon them, the Holy Ghost came on them; and they spake with tongues, and prophesied."

— Acts 19:6

These disciples received the Holy Ghost, spoke with tongues, and prophesied. Again, the experience was definite, recognizable, and connected with spiritual utterance.

THE PATTERN IN ACTS

Together, these passages show that the baptism with the Holy Ghost was not an isolated moment on the Day of Pentecost. The Samaritans received. Saul of Tarsus received. The Gentiles received. The disciples at Ephesus received.

Different places. Different people. Same promise.

The Holy Ghost was given across every boundary: to Jews, to Samaritans, to Gentiles, to a former persecutor of the Church, and to disciples who needed fuller instruction. The promise of the Father was not limited to one place, one people, or one moment in history. It was given to all who would believe and receive.

WHAT JESUS SAID

This pattern should not surprise us. Even before the Day of Pentecost, Jesus said:

"And these signs shall follow them that believe... they shall speak with new tongues."

— Mark 16:17

Speaking in tongues is a sign and evidence that the Spirit is actively working among God's people.

The Spirit gave the utterance, and the believers spoke.

That is the New Testament record.

CHAPTER 5

RECEIVING THE HOLY SPIRIT

Jesus did not present the Holy Spirit as a gift given only to a handful of believers. He spoke of Him as a promise to all whom God would call.

Before His ascension, Jesus said:

"And, behold, I send the promise of my Father upon you..."

— Luke 24:49

Peter also said this promise was to all those called by God:

"Then Peter said unto them, Repent, and be baptized every one of you in the name of Jesus Christ for the remission of sins, and ye shall receive the gift of the Holy Ghost.

For the promise is unto you, and to your children, and to all that are afar off, even as many as the Lord our God shall call."

— Acts 2:38–39

Receiving the Holy Spirit is receiving what God promised to give.

The baptism with the Holy Ghost is not something man invented. It is not a denominational tradition or a teaching created by men. It is the promise of the Father, spoken of by

Jesus, fulfilled in the book of Acts, and made available to believers.

God promised the Holy Spirit to believers because the baptism with the Holy Ghost is good. It is a help and blessing to whosoever will receive it. Jesus spoke ahead of the coming of the Holy Spirit to fill those who believed on Him.

A PROMISE FOR BELIEVERS

The Holy Spirit is not given to the world in this way. He is given to those who belong to Christ.

Jesus said:

"Even the Spirit of truth; whom the world cannot receive, because it seeth him not, neither knoweth him..."

—John 14:17

The world cannot receive Him because the world does not know Him. But the believer can receive because the believer has been made alive unto God.

This is why the question Paul asked in Acts 19 is so important:

"Have ye received the Holy Ghost since ye believed?"

— Acts 19:2

Paul was not asking unbelievers whether they had been saved. He was speaking to disciples. His question shows that receiving the Holy Ghost is something believers should understand, expect, and receive.

The new birth brings us into Christ. The baptism with the Holy Ghost clothes us with power. Both are from God. Both are works of grace. Both are received by faith.

A WILLING AND GRACIOUS FATHER

Jesus also said:

"If ye then, being evil, know how to give good gifts unto your children: how much more shall your heavenly Father give the Holy Spirit to them that ask him?"

— Luke 11:13

God is a willing and gracious Father.

This truth is important because many people approach receiving the Holy Spirit as though God must be persuaded. They wonder whether they are worthy enough, spiritual enough, or prepared enough. But Jesus did not present the Father as stingy or reluctant. He presented Him as a generous Heavenly Father.

A good father does not mock the hunger of his child. A good father does not offer a gift and then pull it away. How much more shall our Heavenly Father give the Holy Spirit to them that ask Him?

The issue is not whether God is willing. The issue is whether we will believe and receive what He has promised.

NOT EARNED, BUT RECEIVED

Receiving the Holy Spirit is not a reward for spiritual achievement. It is not given because a believer has reached a certain level of maturity. It is received by faith.

Salvation is received by faith. Healing is received by faith. The promises of God are received by faith. In the same way, the infilling of the Holy Ghost is received by faith.

There is no need to beg as though God were unwilling. There is no need to strain as though we could force the Spirit of

God to move. There is no need to manufacture emotion in order to make something happen.

We ask.

We believe.

We receive.

The believer does not receive the Holy Ghost because he feels something first. He receives by faith because God has promised to give the Holy Spirit to them that ask Him.

ASK AND RECEIVE

Jesus said the Father gives the Holy Spirit to them that ask Him.

That makes receiving very simple.

A believer may ask the Father for the Holy Ghost with confidence, knowing that the request is according to the will of God. We do not have to wonder whether God wants His people filled with the Spirit. Jesus already settled that.

The book of Acts shows believers receiving in different settings. Some received while someone preached. Some received when hands were laid upon them. Some received in a gathering of believers. The setting may vary, but the promise remains the same.

The important thing is not the outward arrangement. The important thing is faith in the promise of God.

Some have made receiving difficult by giving people too many instructions. Others have made it mysterious, as though only certain kinds of people can receive. But Scripture keeps the matter simple. The Father gives the Holy Spirit to them that ask Him.

A YIELDED RESPONSE

On the Day of Pentecost, the Bible says:

"And they were all filled with the Holy Ghost, and began to speak with other tongues, as the Spirit gave them utterance."

— Acts 2:4

They were filled with the Holy Ghost, and they began to speak.

- The Spirit gave the utterance.
- They did the speaking.

This is an important distinction. The Holy Spirit does not overtake a person in such a way that the believer loses control. He does not force the mouth open. He does not overpower the will. The Spirit does not force people. He leads. He prompts. He gives utterance — the ability to speak as the Spirit directs — and the believer responds by speaking.

That is why receiving the Holy Ghost requires cooperation.

The believer must not try to create the language from the mind. Tongues do not come from the natural understanding. Paul said:

"For if I pray in an unknown tongue, my spirit prayeth, but my understanding is unfruitful."

— 1 Corinthians 14:14

When a believer speaks with tongues, his spirit is praying by the help of the Holy Ghost. The mind may not understand what is being said, but the inner man is actively engaged before God.

This is where some struggle. They wait for God to do the speaking, but Scripture says they spoke as the Spirit gave them utterance. Others try to think of words or form sounds with the mind, but tongues are not produced by mental effort. The believer simply yields to the utterance given by the Spirit and speaks by faith.

DO NOT FEAR

Some believers hesitate because they are afraid of receiving something evil or wrong. Jesus addressed that concern before it ever arose.

He said:

"If a son shall ask bread of any of you that is a father, will he give him a stone? or if he ask a fish, will he for a fish give him a serpent?

Or if he shall ask an egg, will he offer him a scorpion?"

— Luke 11:11–12

Then He said:

"How much more shall your heavenly Father give the Holy Spirit to them that ask him?"

— Luke 11:13

A child of God does not need to be afraid when asking the Father for what Jesus promised. If a believer comes sincerely to God, asking for the Holy Spirit, the Father will not give him something evil. He will give what He promised.

This confidence removes fear. The believer can come boldly, reverently, and simply, knowing the goodness of the Father and trusting God to give what He has promised.

THE PLACE OF LAYING ON OF HANDS

In the book of Acts, believers sometimes received the Holy Ghost through the laying on of hands.

When Paul came to the disciples at Ephesus, Scripture says:

"And when Paul had laid his hands upon them, the Holy

Ghost came on them; and they spake with tongues, and prophesied."

— Acts 19:6

Laying on of hands is biblical. It can help the believer receive, especially when those ministering are full of faith and understand how to lead someone into the baptism with the Holy Ghost.

At the same time, Holy Scripture does not show people being born again through the laying on of hands. The power is not in the hands of man. Both salvation and the gift of the Holy Ghost come from God.

A minister may lay hands on a believer, pray, encourage, and instruct him, but it is the Father who gives the Spirit. The believer receives by faith and yields to the Spirit's utterance.

This keeps our confidence in the right place. We honor ministers and the ministry, but God is the giver and source of every good gift.

SIMPLE CONFIDENCE

Some receive quietly. Others receive with great joy. Some speak only a few words at first. Others begin to speak fluently. The outward expression may vary, but the foundation is always the same: trust in the faithfulness of God to give what He has promised.

A person does not need to compare his experience with another person's experience. The question is not whether it happened exactly the same way it happened for someone else. The question is whether the believer received what God promised and yielded to the Spirit.

The Holy Ghost is not received by personal effort or striving. He is received by faith.

The believer can say, "Father, I ask You to fill me with the Holy Ghost. I believe what You promised. I receive now by faith, and I expect to speak with other tongues as the Spirit gives me utterance."

Then, instead of continuing to speak in his known language, he may respond to the prompting that rises from within and, by faith, speak with other tongues, though the words are unknown to him.

This is simple, but it is not natural. It is supernatural.

A DOORWAY INTO A SPIRIT-FILLED LIFE

Receiving the Holy Ghost is not the end goal or pinnacle of spiritual development. It is a beginning.

God does not fill believers merely so they can say they have had an experience. He fills them so they may live with power, pray with greater help, worship beyond the limits of natural speech, and become more sensitive to the moving of the Spirit.

Speaking with tongues is the initial evidence, but it is also a doorway into a deeper life of prayer in the Spirit, walking with the Spirit, and being used by the Spirit.

A believer who receives the Holy Ghost should continue to pray in tongues. He should not treat the experience as something that happened once and then set it aside. The gift of tongues should be continually used and cultivated. The more a believer prays in the Spirit, the more sensitive he becomes to spiritual things and the more familiar he becomes with a Spirit-filled life.

The apostle Paul stated:

"I thank my God, I speak with tongues more than ye all."

— 1 Corinthians 14:18

That yieldedness matters not only in private prayer, but also in the life of the church. A church filled with believers who know how to yield to the Spirit is better prepared for the manifestations of the Spirit in the public assembly.

WHAT GOD PROMISED, HE IS FAITHFUL TO GIVE

The Father gives life through salvation and power through the infilling of the Holy Ghost. Both are gifts of grace.

The believer does not need to be afraid. He does not need to strive. He does not need to earn what God has promised.

He may ask. He may believe. He may receive. He may yield.

With this understanding, believers can move forward with confidence, knowing that what God has promised, He is faithful to perform.

This prepares us for what comes next. The Holy Ghost not only fills believers for power, prayer, and witness; He also ministers through the body in the gathered church. To understand a Holy Ghost church, we must now look at the manifestations of the Spirit.

PART II
MANIFESTATIONS OF THE SPIRIT

"But the manifestation of the Spirit is given to every man to profit withal."
— 1 Corinthians 12:7

CHAPTER 6

CONCERNING SPIRITUAL GIFTS

When Paul wrote, "Now concerning spiritual gifts," he was not introducing something strange or unreachable. He was addressing spiritual things God wanted the Church to understand.

When we speak of "manifestations of the Spirit," we are simply speaking of ways the Holy Spirit makes Himself known.

The Spirit of God is always present with the believer. He dwells within us. He leads, teaches, comforts, strengthens, and helps us in our walk with God. But there are also times when His working becomes especially evident. In those moments, God is not asking the Church to guess. He is showing Himself.

The word "manifestation" means something made visible, clear, or evident. A manifestation of the Spirit is not the Holy Ghost becoming present for the first time. It is the Holy Ghost making His presence and working known in a particular way.

Paul wrote:

"But the manifestation of the Spirit is given to every man to profit withal."

— 1 Corinthians 12:7

That verse gives us both the nature and the purpose of these manifestations. They are of the Spirit, and they are given to profit. They are sacred operations of the Holy Ghost, given to help people, strengthen believers, and edify the Church.

THE WORD AND THE SPIRIT TOGETHER

Manifestations of the Spirit are not meant to replace the preaching of the Word. They work alongside the Word.

A church should never have to choose between the Word and the Spirit. We need the Word, and we need the Holy Ghost.

The Word gives us the foundation. The Spirit gives strength, direction, conviction, comfort, and power so the Church is built up and Jesus is exalted.

The Word keeps us steady.

The Spirit keeps us alive.

The Word gives light.

The Spirit gives utterance, power, and demonstration.

The Word gives the boundaries.

The Spirit moves within those boundaries according to the will of God.

When the Word is neglected, spiritual activity can become unstable. When the Spirit is ignored, church life can become formal and powerless. But when the Word is honored and the Spirit is welcomed, the Church is strengthened in the way God intended.

This is why a Holy Ghost church must also be a Word church. The Spirit of God will never lead the Church away from the Word He inspired. He will move in line with the Word, confirm the Word, and glorify Jesus.

NOT STRANGE, BUT SCRIPTURAL

Many believers think of spiritual gifts as something complicated, mysterious, or reserved for "special people." Others think of them as something that may happen only in unusual services or during seasons of revival.

But in the New Testament, Paul speaks of these things as part of normal church life.

He did not write to the Corinthians as though manifestations of the Spirit were foreign to the local church. He wrote to teach them how to understand spiritual things and keep them in order.

He began 1 Corinthians 12 by saying:

"Now concerning spiritual gifts, brethren, I would not have you ignorant."

— 1 Corinthians 12:1

God does not want the Church ignorant concerning spiritual things. He wants believers taught. He wants pastors equipped. He wants congregations to understand what the Spirit of God has provided.

Ignorance creates fear.

Knowledge builds confidence.

When people are not taught, they often become afraid of the manifestations of the Spirit or careless with them. Neither is healthy. The answer to ignorance is not silence. The answer is sound teaching from the Word of God.

SUPERNATURAL, YET ORDERLY

These manifestations are entirely supernatural, yet they operate through yielded believers as the Spirit gives utterance, direction, and enablement.

That balance is important.

They do not originate in human ability. A word of knowledge is not natural information. A word of wisdom is not natural advice. The gifts of healing are not natural medicine or medical skill. A tongue with interpretation is not a planned speech. Prophecy is not merely strong encouragement. These manifestations originate with the Spirit of God and are wholly supernatural.

Yet they operate through people.

The Spirit manifests.

The believer yields.

That means spiritual manifestations do not remove responsibility from the believer. The person being used by the Spirit still remains yielded, thoughtful, and subject to the order of God's Word. The Holy Ghost does not produce disorder and then blame it on inspiration. He moves in peace, love, and holiness.

This is why Paul could teach both freedom and order. He could say, "desire spiritual gifts" (1 Corinthians 14:1), and he could also say, "Let all things be done decently and in order" (1 Corinthians 14:40). The two belong together.

A church that welcomes the Spirit should also welcome instruction. A church that desires manifestations should also desire maturity.

THE PURPOSE IS PROFIT

Paul said the manifestation of the Spirit is given "to profit withal" (1 Corinthians 12:7). That means these manifestations are given for benefit.

They help the Church.

They strengthen believers.

They bring direction, comfort, correction, healing, faith, revelation, and utterance as the Spirit wills.

The manifestations of the Spirit are tools of love.

They are not spiritual entertainment. They are not decorations added to a church service. They are not meant to prove that one congregation is better than another. They are given because God loves His people and knows how to help them.

This keeps the motive pure. We desire the manifestations of the Spirit, not because we want something unusual to happen, but because we want people to be helped.

REMOVING UNNECESSARY BARRIERS

Here is the key: a Holy Ghost church does not try to manufacture spiritual activity. It removes unnecessary barriers so the Spirit of God can move as He desires, in the way Scripture permits, and for the purposes Scripture reveals.

A church cannot force the Spirit to manifest.

A pastor cannot schedule a move of God.

A believer cannot manufacture a gift of the Spirit.

But a church can make room.

It can teach the Word clearly.

It can cultivate faith.

It can create an atmosphere of reverence and expectancy.

It can instruct believers so they are not afraid.

It can provide order so people feel safe.

It can give time for the Spirit to move.

It can refuse to shut down what Scripture tells us to desire.

Very often, churches do not resist the Spirit deliberately. They simply leave Him no room to move. Everything is planned so tightly, hurried so quickly, or controlled so carefully that there is little opportunity for the Spirit to minister as He wills.

Order is good. Preparation is good. Structure can serve the purposes of God. But structure must remain a servant, not a master.

A Holy Ghost church does not abandon order. It learns how to make room within order.

EDIFICATION IS THE AIM

The purpose of spiritual manifestations is not merely that something supernatural happen. The purpose is that the Church be edified.

Paul said:

"Let all things be done unto edifying."

— 1 Corinthians 14:26

That one sentence governs the operation of spiritual manifestations in the gathered church. If something does not build up, strengthen, help, or profit the body, it has missed the purpose.

This is why manifestations must be judged by Scripture, received with humility, and handled with care. The question is not merely, "Was something supernatural?" The question is, "Did it edify?"

Did it strengthen the Church?

Did it point people to Jesus?

Did it agree with the Word?

Did it bring peace, clarity, conviction, comfort, or help?

Did it serve the purpose of God?

A true manifestation of the Spirit will not exalt the flesh. It will not draw attention away from Christ. It will not undermine Scripture. It will be consistent with the peace and order of God. The Spirit of God manifests to reveal Jesus, help people, and build up the body.

A CHURCH THAT UNDERSTANDS

A church that understands these things will not be careless with spiritual manifestations, but neither will it be afraid of them.

It will not treat them as toys.

It will not treat them as threats.

It will treat them as sacred operations of the Holy Ghost, given for the profit of the Church.

This is one reason teaching is so important. When believers are taught, fear begins to leave. They learn that the gifts of the Spirit can operate in peace. They learn that the Holy Ghost does not embarrass the Church. They learn that order does not quench the Spirit when order is biblical. They learn that yieldedness and reverence can work together.

A congregation does not become a Holy Ghost church by accident. It must be taught. It must be led. It must be given room to grow.

THE SAFE FOUNDATION

As we continue, we will keep returning to the same safe foundation: God's Word shows us both what the Spirit desires to do and how these manifestations function decently and in order (1 Corinthians 14:40).

The Bible does not leave us with two poor choices: dead formality or uncontrolled excess. Scripture gives us a better way.

The Word honored.

The Spirit welcomed.

Jesus glorified.

The Church edified.

That is the pattern we are seeking.

In the next chapter, we will look at the nine manifestations of the Spirit listed in 1 Corinthians 12. These manifestations are not strange or unreachable. They are God's supernatural help for His people, given by the Spirit, governed by the Word, and intended to strengthen the Church.

CHAPTER 7

THE NINE MANIFESTATIONS OF THE SPIRIT

Paul lists what are often called "the gifts of the Spirit" in 1 Corinthians 12. He writes:

"Now concerning spiritual gifts, brethren, I would not have you ignorant."

— 1 Corinthians 12:1

God does not want the Church uninformed. When believers understand what Scripture says, fear begins to fade and faith begins to rise.

Ignorance has never helped the Church. It causes some to resist what God has provided, and it causes others to mishandle what God has given. But when the Word of God is taught clearly, believers can receive the ministry of the Holy Ghost with confidence, reverence, and order.

Paul did not say, "I would not have you involved."

He said, "I would not have you ignorant" (1 Corinthians 12:1).

That means spiritual things are meant to be understood.

THE LIVING GOD SPEAKS

Paul's opening words in this passage also carry an important contrast. He reminds the Corinthians that before Christ they had been "carried away unto these dumb idols."

"Ye know that ye were Gentiles, carried away unto these dumb idols, even as ye were led."

— 1 Corinthians 12:2

In that context, "dumb" does not mean unintelligent. It means unable to speak.

Idols cannot talk. False gods have nothing to say. They cannot lead, reveal, correct, comfort, direct, or speak life to the people who worship them.

But the Church does not serve a dumb idol.

We serve the living God.

The God of the Bible speaks. He speaks through His written Word. He speaks by His Spirit within the believer. He also makes Himself known in the midst of His people through the manifestations of the Spirit.

That is one of the great differences between the true God and every false god. The living God makes Himself known.

We do not merely speak to God. He also speaks to us by His Word, leads us by His Spirit, and ministers to His people through the manifestations of the Spirit.

This does not mean every spiritual impression is from God. It does not mean every utterance should be received without judgment. The same Bible that teaches us to welcome the Spirit also teaches us to judge spiritual things by the Word.

"Prove all things; hold fast that which is good."

— 1 Thessalonians 5:21

But we must not become so afraid of error that we close ourselves to truth. The answer to false manifestations is not the absence of manifestation. The answer is true manifestation governed by the Word of God.

GIVEN TO PROFIT

Before Paul lists the nine manifestations, he gives their purpose:

"But the manifestation of the Spirit is given to every man to profit withal."

— 1 Corinthians 12:7

These manifestations are given to profit. They are not given for display, entertainment, or self-promotion. They are given to help.

The Church needs help that human wisdom cannot provide. There are times when natural knowledge is not enough. There are moments when ordinary ability cannot meet the need. There are situations where the Church needs revelation, power, or utterance that comes by the Spirit of God.

That is why these manifestations matter.

They are God's supernatural help for His people.

THE NINE MANIFESTATIONS

In 1 Corinthians 12, Paul names nine manifestations of the Spirit:

> "For to one is given by the Spirit the word of wisdom; to another the word of knowledge by the same Spirit;
>
> To another faith by the same Spirit; to another the gifts of healing by the same Spirit;
>
> To another the working of miracles; to another prophecy; to another discerning of spirits; to another divers kinds of tongues; to another the interpretation of tongues:

But all these worketh that one and the selfsame Spirit, dividing to every man severally as he will."

— 1 Corinthians 12:8–11

These manifestations are often grouped into three categories:

Revelation gifts:

The word of wisdom

The word of knowledge

Discerning of spirits

Power gifts:

The gift of faith

Gifts of healing

The working of miracles

Utterance gifts:

Prophecy

Divers kinds of tongues

Interpretation of tongues

Before further defining the nine manifestations one by one, remember how Paul prefaces his list: "Now there are diversities of gifts, but the same Spirit. And there are differences of administrations, but the same Lord. And there are diversities of operations, but it is the same God which worketh all in all" (1 Corinthians 12:4–6). In other words, the Holy Spirit distributes a variety of gifts, the Lord appoints different administrations, and the same God operates in diverse ways. Although this book will give special attention to the nine manifestations, especially prophecy, tongues, and interpretation, it is helpful to note that Paul also speaks of "administrations" and "operations." Administrations include ministry offices such as apostles, prophets, evangelists, pastors, and teachers. Operations refer to the various ways God works through these gifts and ministries. For instance, all evangelists do not operate in exactly the same way. The office may be the same, but the emphasis and operation may differ as the Holy Spirit works through different people in different ways. The same is true of pastors, teachers, and other ministry gifts. All of these come from the same triune God and operate together in His Church. Our focus will be on how the manifestations work within the local assembly.

These groupings are not meant to be technical or rigid. They are simply a helpful way of seeing the different kinds of supernatural help God supplies to His people.

At times the Church needs revelation: light and understanding.

At times the Church needs power: special faith, healings, and miracles.

At times the Church needs utterance: Spirit-inspired speech that brings edification, exhortation, and comfort.

All of these come from the same Spirit. They are different manifestations, but they have one source.

REVELATION GIFTS

The revelation gifts reveal something.

They do not make a person all-knowing. They do not make someone a fortune teller. They do not give a believer the right to pry into another person's life. They are not natural suspicion or human perception dressed up in spiritual language.

They are moments when the Spirit of God reveals what needs to be known for the purpose of helping His people.

The word of wisdom is a supernatural revelation concerning the wisdom, plan, or purpose of God. It often gives direction. It may reveal what should be done, how something should be handled, or what God intends in a situation.

The word of knowledge is a supernatural revelation of facts known to God but not known naturally by the person ministering. It may uncover a condition, a need, a circumstance, or something God wants brought to light.

Discerning of spirits is supernatural insight into the realm of spirits. It is not the gift of suspicion. It is not the gift of criticism. It is not the ability to discern people's faults. It is a manifestation by which the Spirit of God enables a person to recognize the presence or activity of a spirit, whether divine, human, or evil.

These manifestations are given because God sees what we cannot see and knows what we cannot know naturally.

POWER GIFTS

The power gifts do something.

They are demonstrations of the power of God beyond natural ability.

The gift of faith is a special manifestation of faith given by the Spirit for a particular situation. It is not the general faith by which every believer lives. It is a supernatural endowment of faith that enables a person to receive from God or minister blessing to others according to the will of God. The gift of faith acts and speaks with unusual confidence in the power and promise of God.

The gifts of healing are manifestations of the Spirit by which God ministers healing to the sick. The plural expression is important. Scripture says "gifts of healing" (1 Corinthians 12:9), which points to the many ways and many kinds of healings God may work by His Spirit.

The working of miracles is a manifestation of divine power that interrupts the ordinary course of nature or circumstances.

It is God working in a way that cannot be explained by natural means.

These manifestations remind us that the gospel was never meant to be preached in word only. Paul said:

"And my speech and my preaching was not with enticing words of man's wisdom, but in demonstration of the Spirit and of power."

— 1 Corinthians 2:4

The early Church preached the Word, and God confirmed His Word. The same Holy Ghost who gave boldness to preach also demonstrated the reality of the risen Christ.

UTTERANCE GIFTS

The utterance gifts say something.

They are manifestations of the Spirit through Spirit-inspired speech.

Prophecy is a supernatural utterance in a known tongue. In its simple New Testament use, prophecy speaks unto men to edification, exhortation, and comfort (1 Corinthians 14:3).

Divers kinds of tongues are supernatural utterances in languages unknown to the speaker. In private prayer, tongues are Godward and strengthen the believer. In the public assembly, a tongue is to be interpreted so the Church may receive understanding and edification.

Interpretation of tongues is the supernatural showing forth of the meaning of an utterance given in tongues. It is not translation in the ordinary sense. It is the Spirit-given interpretation of what has been spoken, so that the congregation may be edified.

These utterance gifts are especially important to the theme of this book because they show how the living God speaks in the gathered church. They remind us that a New Testament service was never intended to be only one person speaking and everyone else listening. There is order. There is leadership. There is preaching and teaching. But there is also room for the Spirit to minister through the body.

TOOLS OF LOVE

We do not have to over-explain each manifestation in this part of the book. The main point is this: God has provided supernatural help for the local church.

These manifestations are not decorations. They are tools of love.

A word of wisdom can bring direction.

A word of knowledge can reveal a need.

Discerning of spirits can bring clarity.

Special faith can lift a congregation beyond fear.

Gifts of healing can minister life to the sick.

The working of miracles can display the power of God.

Prophecy can edify, exhort, and comfort.

Tongues with interpretation can bring a present word to the congregation.

All of these are given so people can be helped and the body of Christ can be strengthened.

If love is our motive, we will not despise the manifestations of the Spirit. We will desire what God has provided for the profit of His people.

THE SPIRIT DIVIDES AS HE WILLS

Paul closes the list by saying:

"But all these worketh that one and the selfsame Spirit, dividing to every man severally as he will."

— 1 Corinthians 12:11

This keeps the Church humble.

The manifestations belong to the Spirit. He is the One who distributes them. No believer possesses a gift of the Spirit in such a way that he can operate it apart from God's will and direction.

At the same time, believers filled with the Holy Ghost may speak in tongues freely in personal devotion, prayer, worship, and spiritual edification, whether privately or at appropriate times in public worship. The apostle Paul said, "I will pray with the spirit, and I will pray with the understanding also" (1 Corinthians 14:15). His words show that the believer's will is involved. Later he testified, "I thank my God, I speak with tongues more than ye all" (1 Corinthians 14:18). Paul clearly valued and practiced speaking with tongues, but he also made a distinction between speaking to God in tongues and speaking to the gathered church with a tongue that must be interpreted.

Tongues are spoken as the believer yields to the Holy Spirit and speaks by the utterance He gives. The distinction is not in the source, but in the setting, purpose, and order. A tongue addressed to the assembly is governed by the unction of the Spirit and the order of Scripture.

Never is a person forced to speak publicly in tongues against his will. Paul said, "If any man speak in an unknown tongue..." (1 Corinthians 14:27). The word "if" shows that the speaker's own will is involved. He may yield, or he may refrain. Yet when tongues are brought into the gathered assembly as a public utterance, they must be governed by the unction of the Spirit and by the order Paul gives: "by two, or at the most by three, and that by course; and let one interpret" (1 Corinthians 14:27).

The Spirit wills, the believer yields, and the church follows the order of Scripture.

We yield.

He manifests.

We desire spiritual gifts.

He divides as He wills.

We make room.

He supplies.

This truth protects us from pride, pressure, and performance. A Holy Ghost church does not try to force manifestations. It remains hungry, reverent, taught, yielded, and ready.

WHY THIS MATTERS TO THE LOCAL CHURCH

The local church needs the manifestations of the Spirit because the local church needs the help of the Spirit.

Human talent cannot replace revelation.

Programs cannot replace power.

Organization cannot replace utterance.

Good intentions cannot replace the present ministry of the Holy Ghost.

This does not mean we despise preparation, leadership, planning, or structure. Those things can serve the purposes of God. But they must never become substitutes for the Spirit of God.

A church may have strong preaching and still need the manifestations of the Spirit.

A church may have good music and still need the manifestations of the Spirit.

A church may have sound doctrine and still need the manifestations of the Spirit.

The Word gives us truth. The Spirit confirms, applies, and manifests that truth among the people.

A church should never have to choose between being scriptural and being spiritual. The New Testament pattern is both.

LOOKING AHEAD

As we go further, we will give special attention to tongues and interpretation, because they clearly show how the Spirit works through the members of the body together.

A public tongue requires yielding.

Interpretation requires yielding.

The congregation receives profit.

The body is edified.

Jesus is glorified.

That is the beauty of a Holy Ghost church.

The living God speaks.

The Spirit manifests.

The Church is strengthened.

And all of it is to be done in love, according to the Word, and for the glory of God.

CHAPTER 8

HOW THE SPIRIT DISTRIBUTES AND HOW THE CHURCH RESPONDS

One of the most important truths a church can learn is that the manifestations of the Spirit belong to the Spirit. They do not begin with man, and they are not controlled by man. The Spirit of God is the One who distributes them as He wills.

Paul says:

"But all these worketh that one and the selfsame Spirit, dividing to every man severally as he will."

— 1 Corinthians 12:11

This teaches humility.

The manifestations of the Spirit belong to the Spirit. They do not belong to the preacher, the pastor, the prophet, the congregation, or the person through whom they may operate. The Spirit is the source. He is the giver. He divides to every man severally as He wills.

This means we do not control the Spirit. We do not command Him, schedule Him, or manufacture His manifestations. The Holy Ghost is God. He is not a force to be managed or an atmosphere to be produced. He is the Spirit of the living God, and He manifests as He wills.

But this truth must be handled carefully. The fact that the Spirit divides as He wills does not mean the Church should become passive.

NOT CONTROL, BUT COOPERATION

Some have taken the words "as he will" (1 Corinthians 12:11) and used them to explain why nothing supernatural ever happens. They say, "If God wants to move, He will move." There is truth in that statement, but it can also become an excuse for unbelief, neglect, or spiritual laziness.

Scripture shows both sides.

The Spirit gives as He wills.

The Church is commanded to desire spiritual gifts.

Paul later says:

"But covet earnestly the best gifts..."

— 1 Corinthians 12:31

And again:

"Follow after charity, and desire spiritual gifts..."

— 1 Corinthians 14:1

So here is the balance: we cannot force the Spirit, but we can welcome Him. We cannot manufacture manifestations, but we can make room for them. We cannot work up a move of God, but we can cultivate faith, hunger, reverence, and order so that when the Spirit begins to move, the Church recognizes it and responds properly.

The Spirit's sovereignty does not cancel the Church's responsibility.

DESIRE IS BIBLICAL

Paul did not tell the Church to ignore spiritual gifts. He told the Church to desire them.

That word matters.

Desire is not presumption.

Desire is not control.

Desire is not emotional excess.

Desire is the proper response of a heart that believes God's Word and values what God has provided.

If the manifestation of the Spirit is given to profit, then love will desire that profit for the Church. If prophecy edifies, exhorts, and comforts, then love will desire prophecy. If tongues with interpretation edifies the Church, then love will desire that operation in its proper place. If gifts of healing minister to the sick, then love will desire the sick to be helped.

The motive is not curiosity. The motive is love.

This is why Paul says, "Follow after charity, and desire spiritual gifts" (1 Corinthians 14:1). Love comes first. Spiritual desire must be governed by love. We do not desire manifestations so we can appear spiritual. We desire them because people need help.

A church without desire will usually become a church without manifestation. Not because God is unwilling, but because the church has made little room for what He told it to desire.

PASSIVITY IS NOT SPIRITUAL

Passivity can sound humble, but it is not always faith.

A person may say, "If God wants to use me, He will." But the Bible teaches believers to yield, pray, desire, and obey. The Spirit gives the utterance, but the believer speaks. The Spirit gives the manifestation, but the believer yields. The Spirit distributes as He wills, but the Church desires and makes room.

This is not human effort replacing divine operation. It is human obedience cooperating with divine operation.

On the Day of Pentecost, the disciples did not create the rushing mighty wind. They did not create the cloven tongues like as of fire. They did not invent the languages. But when the Spirit gave utterance, they began to speak.

That is cooperation.

The Spirit moved.

They responded.

A Holy Ghost church learns to respond.

WE CANNOT WORK IT UP

There is another ditch on the opposite side.

Some, in trying to make room for the Spirit, begin to pressure people, force moments, or confuse emotion with manifestation. But the Spirit of God does not need fleshly assistance.

A church cannot work up a word of knowledge.

A believer cannot work up a gift of healing.

A pastor cannot work up tongues and interpretation.

A congregation cannot work up prophecy by emotional pressure.

The flesh may imitate, but only the Spirit can manifest.

This is why reverence matters. A true move of the Spirit is not something to be played with. We do not need to exaggerate, perform, or pretend. If the Spirit manifests, we receive it with gratitude. If He does not manifest in a particular way at a particular moment, we do not force it.

Faith does not pretend.

Faith trusts.

A Holy Ghost church is not a theatrical church. It is a yielded church.

MAKING ROOM

Making room for the Spirit is different from manufacturing spiritual activity.

A church makes room by teaching the Word clearly, encouraging believers to be filled with the Spirit, allowing moments of waiting upon the Lord, honoring spiritual utterance when it occurs in order, and refusing to forbid what Scripture tells us to desire.

This kind of preparation does not control the Spirit. It simply creates an atmosphere where believers are more ready to recognize and respond to Him.

If a church never teaches on the manifestations of the Spirit, people will not know what to do when the Spirit prompts them. If a church never gives any room in the service, even yielded believers may remain silent because they assume there is no place for spiritual utterance.

Making room is part of shepherding.

LEADERSHIP AND THE BODY

Leadership matters because leadership helps set the spiritual tone of the house. A pastor should not resist the Spirit, but neither should he allow disorder in the name of liberty. The shepherd helps the congregation understand both freedom and boundaries.

What is welcomed becomes normal.

What is ignored becomes rare.

What is taught becomes clearer.

What is modeled becomes safer.

At the same time, the manifestations of the Spirit do not belong only to the platform. Paul said the manifestation of the Spirit is given "to every man to profit withal" (1 Corinthians 12:7). That means the body matters.

One may give a tongue.

Another may interpret.

One may prophesy.

Another may judge.

One may receive a word of wisdom.

Another may be strengthened by it.

The Spirit works through members of the body for the good of the whole body.

This does not mean everyone speaks whenever they want. It does not mean the service becomes disorderly or uncontrolled. But it does mean the congregation should be taught that the Holy Ghost may use yielded believers as He wills.

A Holy Ghost church is not a spectator church. It is a body.

THE BALANCE WE MUST KEEP

When a church learns this balance, something beautiful happens. Spiritual hunger awakens. Confidence grows. Fear begins to leave. Believers become more willing to yield, and the congregation begins to understand what is happening and why it matters.

The Spirit's work can be received with greater understanding and handled with greater care among God's people, not because man has taken control, but because the Word is giving order. Not because the church has learned to manufacture manifestations, but because it has learned to make room for the Spirit and respond when He moves.

The balance is simple, but it must be guarded.

The Spirit divides as He wills.

The Church desires spiritual gifts.

The Spirit manifests.

The believer yields.

The Church cannot manufacture.

The Church can make room.

Leadership does not control the Holy Ghost.

Leadership does shepherd the congregation.

Freedom does not mean disorder.

Order does not mean lifelessness.

This is the way of a Holy Ghost church: humble before the sovereignty of the Spirit, obedient to the instruction of Scripture, hungry for what God has provided, and willing to respond when He makes Himself known.

CHAPTER 9

MAKING ROOM FOR THE SPIRIT

When the Spirit begins to move in a church, it is usually because room has been made for Him.

The Holy Spirit is not an intruder. He does not force Himself into a congregation. But where He is honored, heeded, and given room, His activity becomes increasingly evident.

A Holy Ghost church is not built in a single service. It is cultivated over time. As teaching becomes clear and faith grows, the congregation learns to recognize the Spirit and respond when He prompts.

CULTIVATING EXPECTATION

Expectation changes the atmosphere. If a church settles for empty routine, it will usually experience little more than that. But when believers gather with quiet confidence that God is present and willing to move, hearts become attentive and faith rises.

This kind of expectation is not emotional pressure. It is not an attempt to force something to happen. It is the confidence that God is among His people and that the Holy Ghost still ministers according to the Word.

A congregation can be trained to expect the Spirit's help.

They can expect the Word to be preached.

They can expect Jesus to be glorified.

They can expect believers to be strengthened.

They can expect the gifts of the Spirit to operate as He wills.

They can expect God to speak, guide, comfort, correct, and confirm His Word.

Expectation does not control the Spirit, but it prepares the heart to recognize Him.

LEADERSHIP SETS THE TONE

The spiritual posture of leadership helps shape the atmosphere of the church.

A church will rarely move beyond what its shepherd is willing to embrace. This is not about personality. It is about posture.

When leadership is grounded in the Word and open to the Spirit, believers sense that safety. They know the pastor is not trying to manufacture spiritual activity, but they also know he is not afraid of the Holy Ghost.

That matters.

People are often willing to yield, but they need to know there is room to do so. If the atmosphere of the church communicates that spiritual utterance is unwelcome, most believers will remain silent even if the Spirit prompts them. If the atmosphere is careless, people may speak without wisdom. But when leadership teaches, guides, and makes room in peace, the congregation can grow in confidence.

A pastor does not have to make something happen. He

simply has to shepherd the house in such a way that the Spirit is not crowded out.

BEGIN WITH TEACHING

If a congregation is unfamiliar with the manifestations of the Spirit, the first step is not to force public expression. The first step is to teach.

Many believers are not rebellious. They are uninformed. They may love God, honor Scripture, and desire His will, yet still be uncertain about the gifts of the Spirit. Some have seen misuse. Some have heard confusing teaching. Some have never been taught the difference between private prayer in tongues and a public utterance that requires interpretation.

Understanding brings confidence.

A pastor may begin simply by opening the Scriptures and teaching what Paul taught. He may show the congregation that the manifestation of the Spirit is given "to profit withal" (1 Corinthians 12:7). He may explain that tongues, interpretation, prophecy, revelation, and spiritual utterance are not strange additions to church life, but part of the New Testament pattern when handled in order.

He does not need to begin by announcing a dramatic change in the service. He can begin by helping the people see what the Bible says.

Teaching removes fear. It gives people language. It gives them confidence. It shows them that the Holy Ghost does not embarrass the Church, and that the gifts of the Spirit are safe when governed by the Word.

A taught congregation is a safer congregation.

GIVE THE SPIRIT ROOM IN THE SERVICE

A church can believe in the manifestations of the Spirit and still leave no practical room for them.

If every moment is hurried, if every transition is filled, and if every service is so tightly controlled that no pause is allowed, the congregation may never learn to wait upon the Lord.

Making room does not require disorder. It may be as simple as allowing a quiet moment after worship. It may mean waiting briefly before moving to the next part of the service. It may mean the pastor saying, "Let us wait on the Lord for a moment," and then allowing the congregation to become still and attentive.

Waiting does not have to be long to be meaningful. Sometimes even a short pause can lift the level of expectancy in a room.

The point is not to create awkward silence. The point is to give place to the Spirit.

A church can be orderly and still be open. It can have structure and still have sensitivity. It can prepare the service and still allow the Holy Ghost to move.

WHAT A PASTOR MAY SAY

Sometimes leaders want to make room for the Spirit, but they are unsure what to say. They do not want to make the moment awkward, and they do not want to pressure the congregation.

A pastor may speak simply.

He might say:

"Let us wait on the Lord for a moment. We are not trying to force anything. We are simply giving room for the Holy Ghost to minister as He wills."

Or he might say:

"If the Spirit of God is prompting you with a tongue, a word of exhortation, or another utterance, remain reverent and sensitive. We want everything to be done unto edifying and in order."

Or he might say:

"When we come together, Scripture shows that the Holy Ghost may minister through a psalm, doctrine, tongue, revelation, or interpretation. We are going to take a moment and give room for the Spirit to move according to the Word."

Such language helps the congregation understand the moment. It removes pressure without lowering expectation. It teaches while it leads.

The pastor is not required to give a long explanation every time. But especially when a church is learning, a few clear words can help people feel safe and know how to respond.

YIELDED PEOPLE MAKE ROOM

Yielded people make room for the Holy Spirit.

The precious Spirit of God often prompts quietly, and in those moments yieldedness matters. Sometimes the difference between an ordinary service and a deeply meaningful one is the willingness of believers to respond to the Holy Ghost in faith and order.

Yieldedness does not mean every person speaks out whenever he senses something. True yieldedness also stays submitted to the order of the house.

Where a public tongue is given, interpretation must be handled according to the order of Scripture. Where prophecy is given, it must be spoken and judged according to the order of Scripture. The gifts of the Spirit are holy, and they should be handled with reverence, humility, and care.

Sometimes yieldedness means speaking. Sometimes yieldedness means waiting. Sometimes yieldedness means submitting what one senses to leadership before speaking publicly.

A Holy Ghost church must be full of yielded people, not merely excited people.

Excitement may come and go. Yieldedness can be taught, cultivated, and strengthened.

REMOVE UNNECESSARY BARRIERS

A Holy Ghost church does not try to manufacture spiritual activity. It removes unnecessary barriers so that the Spirit of God can minister among His people.

Some barriers are doctrinal. People have been taught that the gifts have passed away or that tongues should never be heard in church.

Some barriers are emotional. People are afraid of being embarrassed or of doing something wrong.

Some barriers are practical. There is simply no room in the service for anything beyond the planned order.

Some barriers are pastoral. Leadership may not know how to guide the congregation in spiritual things.

These barriers can be removed patiently.

Teach the Word.

Encourage prayer in the Spirit.

Make room to wait upon the Lord.

Explain public utterance and interpretation.

Maintain order without shutting down liberty.

Model reverence and confidence.

Over time, the church begins to understand.

TRUST GOD TO DO WHAT ONLY HE CAN DO

There is peace in knowing that we cannot do the Holy Ghost's part.

We can teach.

We can pray.

We can desire.

We can make room.

We can yield.

We can obey.

But only the Spirit can manifest.

This keeps the church from pressure. We are not trying to produce a moment. We are honoring God, obeying Scripture, and trusting the Holy Ghost to minister as He wills.

A Holy Ghost church honors the Word, welcomes the Spirit, and trusts God to do what only He can do.

It does not force.

It does not fear.

It makes room.

And where the Spirit is welcomed in faith, reverence, and order, His activity becomes increasingly evident among the people of God.

CHAPTER 10

ORDER IN THE HOUSE OF GOD

A genuine move of the Spirit is never separated from a willingness to understand and apply the Scriptures. God has not left the Church to guess how spiritual manifestations should function. His Word provides both freedom and guidance so that the work of the Spirit strengthens rather than unsettles the congregation.

In 1 Corinthians 14, Paul uses the words "church" and "churches" nine times. That alone should get our attention. This chapter is not merely about private devotion or personal experience. Paul is dealing with the gathered church. He addresses tongues, interpretation, prophecy, edification, order, and how spiritual utterance should function when believers come together. If Paul gives this much instruction about tongues and interpretation in a chapter so clearly centered on the church, then why would we remove from the life of the church the very things Paul took time to regulate?

Paul wrote:

"How is it then, brethren? when ye come together, every one

of you hath a psalm, hath a doctrine, hath a tongue, hath a revelation, hath an interpretation. Let all things be done unto edifying."

— 1 Corinthians 14:26

PAUL ANSWERS THE PRACTICAL QUESTIONS

First Corinthians 14 is one of the most practical chapters in the New Testament concerning the operation of spiritual utterance in the gathered church. Paul does not leave the church to guess about these matters. He answers the practical questions.

Who may speak?

What should be spoken?

When should a person speak?

Where does this instruction apply?

Why should spiritual utterance be given?

How should it be handled in the assembly?

These are the basic questions that must be answered if a church is going to make room for the Holy Ghost in a scriptural way. Paul answers them with remarkable clarity, not by removing spiritual utterance from the church, but by showing how it is to function in the church. He shows us that spiritual utterance belongs in the gathered assembly, but it must be governed by love, understanding, edification, and order.

This is important because a Holy Ghost church is not a church where anything goes. It is a church where the Spirit is welcomed and the Word is obeyed. Paul does not give these instructions to remove spiritual utterance from the church. He gives them so tongues, interpretation, and prophecy may operate in a way that strengthens the body and honors God.

Most churches understand psalms and doctrine. They

understand worship and teaching. But Paul also speaks of a tongue, a revelation, and an interpretation, then gives one simple rule: "Let all things be done unto edifying" (1 Corinthians 14:26).

The goal is the strengthening of the body.

This verse is important because Paul is describing what may be present when believers come together. He does not treat spiritual utterance as foreign to the gathering. He places it among the normal ingredients of church life, then gives order so that everything strengthens the people.

FREEDOM WITH BOUNDARIES

Paul then gives clear boundaries:

"If any man speak in an unknown tongue, let it be by two, or at the most by three... and let one interpret."

— 1 Corinthians 14:27

"But if there be no interpreter, let him keep silence in the church; and let him speak to himself, and to God."

— 1 Corinthians 14:28

This is not restriction for its own sake. It is protection.

Order is not the enemy of the Spirit. Order protects what the Spirit desires to do.

Paul did not forbid tongues in the church. He regulated their public use so the congregation could be edified. A public tongue should not remain a mystery to the people. It should be interpreted so the Church may receive understanding.

This is one reason a church must be taught. If people do not understand the difference between private prayer in tongues and a public utterance in tongues, confusion can easily arise. In private prayer, a believer may speak to God in tongues and be personally edified. In the public assembly, however, a tongue addressed to the congregation should be interpreted so all may be edified.

The same Spirit is at work, but the setting determines the order.

BY TWO OR THREE

Paul gives clear order for public tongues in the gathered church:

"If any man speak in an unknown tongue, let it be by two, or at the most by three, and that by course; and let one interpret."

— 1 Corinthians 14:27

This means public utterance in tongues should not dominate the service. The Spirit of God is purposeful. He does not need endless repetition to say what He desires to say.

Paul's instruction appears to limit the number of speakers, not merely the number of phrases or utterances. In other words, two or three individuals may be used publicly in tongues in a service, and each tongue should be interpreted. One person may give a tongue and continue until the Spirit's utterance is complete. But once that person has finished, and the service has moved on to another speaker or another part of the flow, he should not keep returning to give additional public tongues.

The point is not to bind the Spirit, but to preserve clarity. Public tongues are not unlimited in a gathering. Two or three speakers are sufficient. This keeps the service from becoming heavy, confusing, or centered on manifestation instead of edification.

The purpose of the gift is not to fill time. The purpose is to help the Church.

BY COURSE

Paul also says, "and that by course."

That means one at a time.

The Spirit does not create competition between voices. If two people speak over one another, the congregation cannot receive clearly. Order allows the message to be heard, interpreted, and judged.

A person may be prompted by the Spirit and still need to wait. Yieldedness includes patience. The ability to speak does not remove the responsibility to do so in order.

Sometimes the most spiritual thing a believer can do is hold steady until the proper moment.

LET ONE INTERPRET

Paul then says, "and let one interpret."

This instruction brings clarity. A public tongue should be followed by interpretation so the congregation can understand and receive benefit.

There may be more than one person in a church who is capable of interpreting, but in the public operation of tongues and interpretation, there should be order. The tongue is not to be followed by several competing interpretations. One person should interpret so the congregation can receive clearly.

This does not mean the same person can never give both the tongue and the interpretation. Paul also says:

"Wherefore let him that speaketh in an unknown tongue pray that he may interpret."

— 1 Corinthians 14:13

So Scripture allows for that possibility. Yet verse 28 also shows that the person who gives the tongue is not automatically obligated to interpret that tongue. He may not be equipped or prepared to give the interpretation, and that is not wrong. The important thing is that an interpreter must be present if the tongue is to function publicly for the edification of the congregation.

In some churches, there may be a person known by leadership to be used regularly in interpretation. In other settings, the same person who gives the tongue may interpret. The important thing is not personal display, but the edifying of the body.

IF THERE IS NO INTERPRETER

Paul says:

"But if there be no interpreter, let him keep silence in the church; and let him speak to himself, and to God."

— 1 Corinthians 14:28

This is one of the most helpful instructions in the chapter.

Paul's statement assumes that the presence or absence of an interpreter can be recognized. If there is no interpreter present, or if no recognized interpretation is forthcoming, the tongue should not continue as a public utterance to the congregation.

Paul does not say the person is wrong for having a tongue. He does not say the person is unspiritual. He simply gives order. If there is no interpreter, the utterance should not be given publicly to the congregation.

The believer may still speak to himself and to God. There is still prayer. There is still communion. There is still spiritual life. But the public message waits until interpretation can bring understanding to all.

This protects the congregation without despising the gift.

INSTRUCTING WITHOUT EMBARRASSING

A pastor should teach these things before there is a problem. It is much easier to guide a congregation when the people already understand the order of Scripture.

A pastor might say publicly:

"If you sense that you have a tongue or interpretation, remain reverent and sensitive. We want to make room for the Spirit, but we also want all things done unto edifying. If you are unsure, wait. The Holy Ghost will not be offended by order."

Or he might say:

"If you are new to this church, or if you are unsure how spiritual utterance is handled here, please speak with leadership. We want to encourage the gifts of the Spirit, and we also want to preserve the peace and order of the house."

This kind of instruction does not quench the Spirit. It helps people understand how to respond.

If someone speaks out of turn or acts unwisely, the pastor does not need to shame the person publicly. If the moment must be addressed, it can be addressed gently and briefly. Much correction can happen privately afterward.

A simple public statement may be enough:

"We appreciate every sincere desire to obey the Lord. We also want to keep everything in order so the whole church can be edified."

That preserves dignity while protecting the congregation.

THE ARK AND DUE ORDER

The Old Testament gives a vivid picture of this principle in David's first attempt to bring the ark of God to Jerusalem.

The ark of God represented the presence of God among His

people. It was not an ordinary piece of furniture. It was holy. It was sacred. It was connected with the covenant, the mercy seat, and the manifest presence of God in Israel.

Years before David became king, the Philistines captured the ark and carried it from Ebenezer to Ashdod. They brought it into the house of Dagon and set it beside their idol.

"And the Philistines took the ark of God, and brought it from Ebenezer unto Ashdod.

When the Philistines took the ark of God, they brought it into the house of Dagon, and set it by Dagon."

— 1 Samuel 5:1–2

But the ark did not belong in the house of Dagon. The presence of God could not be treated as though it were common. Judgment and trouble followed the Philistines wherever the ark went. Ashdod was troubled. Gath was troubled. Ekron was troubled. The hand of the Lord was heavy upon them.

After seven months, the Philistines decided to send the ark back to Israel. They placed it on a new cart and sent it away.

"Now therefore make a new cart, and take two milch kine, on which there hath come no yoke, and tie the kine to the cart, and bring their calves home from them:

And take the ark of the LORD, and lay it upon the cart..."

— 1 Samuel 6:7–8

That was the Philistine way of moving the ark. They did not know the law of God. They did not have the written instruction given to Israel. They did what seemed reasonable to them.

But later, when David became king and desired to bring the ark to Jerusalem, he made a serious mistake. He had a right desire, but he followed the wrong pattern.

"And they carried the ark of God in a new cart out of the house of Abinadab..."

— 1 Chronicles 13:7

David wanted the ark. He wanted the presence of God restored to its rightful place among the people of God. His desire was not wrong. But instead of seeking the Word of God concerning how the ark was to be carried, he followed the pattern the Philistines had used. He placed the ark on a new cart.

The Philistines acted according to what seemed reasonable to them. But Israel could not take its pattern from the Philistines, because Israel had the Word of God. In the same way, the church must not assume that what works in the world is automatically acceptable in the house of God.

As the ark was being transported, Uzza put forth his hand to steady it, and judgment fell.

"And the anger of the LORD was kindled against Uzza, and he smote him, because he put his hand to the ark: and there he died before God."

— 1 Chronicles 13:10

The Bible then says:

"And David was displeased, because the LORD had made a breach upon Uzza: wherefore that place is called Perezuzza to this day.

And David was afraid of God that day, saying, How shall I bring the ark of God home to me?"

— 1 Chronicles 13:11–12

David's reaction is very instructive. He was displeased. Then he was afraid. He still wanted the ark, but now he was uncertain about how to bring it home.

Many pastors and leaders have felt something similar concerning the moving of the Holy Ghost. They want the presence of God. They believe in the power of God. They do not want a dead church. But somewhere along the way, they saw confusion, excess, disorder, or trouble, and fear entered their hearts.

Their desire may not be to resist God. Often, their desire is to protect the people. But fear is not the answer. Neglect is not the answer. Removing the ark is not the answer.

The answer is to return to the Word of God and find the due order.

That is exactly what David did.

PROPHECY AND JUDGMENT

Paul also speaks of prophecy in the church:

"Let the prophets speak two or three, and let the other judge.

If any thing be revealed to another that sitteth by, let the first hold his peace.

For ye may all prophesy one by one, that all may learn, and all may be comforted.

And the spirits of the prophets are subject to the prophets.

For God is not the author of confusion, but of peace, as in all churches of the saints."

— 1 Corinthians 14:29–33

Prophecy is to be welcomed, but it is also to be judged. Judging does not mean criticizing harshly. It means weighing what is spoken by the Word of God, by the witness of the Spirit, and by the oversight of mature leadership.

No utterance should be received simply because someone says, "Thus saith the Lord." The Church is not called to be gullible. It is called to be spiritual. The Word judges all things. The Spirit bears witness to truth. Leadership helps guard the peace of the congregation.

Paul also says, "the spirits of the prophets are subject to the prophets" (1 Corinthians 14:32). That means spiritual influence does not remove responsibility. The Holy Ghost does not take control of a person in such a way that self-control disappears.

The Spirit leads.

He does not drive.

A believer can wait. A believer can speak in order. A believer can remain quiet if the situation requires it. This truth brings peace to the church. The congregation does not need to fear the manifestations of the Spirit, because the Spirit of God does not produce confusion. He works in harmony with His Word.

ORDER PROTECTS LIBERTY

Where God is guiding, peace follows.

Order is not lifelessness. Order is not unbelief. Order is not control. Biblical order gives the Spirit's work a safe channel through which to bless the Church.

A river without banks becomes a flood. But a river with banks can flow with strength and direction. So it is with the move of the Spirit. The banks are not there to stop the river. They are there so the river can bless what it touches.

God has given the Church both liberty and instruction. We do not have to choose between them.

The Spirit gives life.

The Word gives order.

Together, the Church is edified.

When a church learns this, fear begins to leave. Leaders no longer have to choose between openness and safety. Believers no longer have to choose between yieldedness and restraint.

The Spirit moves, and the Church is at peace.

This is order in the house of God.

CHAPTER 11

SHEPHERDING THE FLOW

When the Spirit begins to move in a church, wise leadership becomes more important, not less. A genuine move of God does not remove the need for shepherding; it increases it. The same Spirit who manifests His presence is also the One who appoints leadership within the Church so that His work may strengthen the body rather than unsettle it.

Spiritual leadership was never designed to control the activity of God, but neither was it meant to stand aside without discernment. Scripture presents leadership as a gift to the Church, providing direction, care, and protection as believers grow together. A pastor does not replace the work of the Spirit. A pastor helps steward what God is doing.

Every local church is a spiritual household. When leadership remains grounded in the Word and sensitive to the Spirit, believers feel safe. They understand that spiritual expressions will be received with wisdom and guided with care.

LEADERSHIP PROVIDES SAFETY

A church that welcomes the Holy Ghost must also value spiritual safety. Safety does not mean fear. It does not mean control. It means the congregation knows that what happens in the service will be handled according to the Word, in peace, and for edification.

Paul instructed the church:

"Let the prophets speak two or three, and let the other judge."

— 1 Corinthians 14:29

Judging does not mean harsh criticism. It means weighing what is spoken so that the Church remains anchored in truth.

Then Paul gives a stabilizing truth:

"And the spirits of the prophets are subject to the prophets."

— 1 Corinthians 14:32

In other words, spiritual influence never removes personal responsibility. A believer is not overtaken in such a way that self-control disappears.

And Paul concludes:

"For God is not the author of confusion, but of peace, as in all churches of the saints."

— 1 Corinthians 14:33

A pastor helps provide safety by teaching clearly, leading calmly, and correcting wisely when correction is needed. If the congregation senses that leadership is afraid, the people may become hesitant. If leadership is careless, the people may become confused. But when leadership is steady, Word-governed, and open to the Spirit, the church can grow in confidence.

TEACH BEFORE YOU CORRECT

One of the best ways to shepherd spiritual manifestations is to teach before problems arise.

Many people who make mistakes are not rebellious. They are simply uninformed. A person may sincerely feel prompted by the Spirit and still not know how to respond in order.

For this reason, pastors should not wait until something goes wrong to explain spiritual order. They can teach the congregation what Scripture says about tongues, interpretation, prophecy, judging, waiting, and doing all things unto edifying.

A pastor may say:

"We want to make room for the Holy Ghost in this church. We also want everything to be done according to the Word, in peace, and for the strengthening of the body."

That simple kind of instruction helps the congregation understand both liberty and order.

CORRECT WITHOUT CRUSHING

Correction should not be harsh when the heart is sincere.

If someone speaks out of turn, gives something that does not edify, or misunderstands the prompting of the Spirit, the pastor should handle it with wisdom. Not every mistake needs a public rebuke. Often, a private conversation after the service is better.

A pastor might say privately:

"I appreciate your desire to obey the Lord. Let me help you understand how we handle spiritual utterance in this church so it can bring the most edification."

That kind of correction preserves dignity while still giving direction.

There may be times when something must be addressed

publicly for the sake of the congregation. Even then, the tone should be calm, not humiliating. The goal is not to embarrass the person. The goal is to protect the peace of the house and the edification of the body.

A pastor can be firm without being severe. He can guard the service without wounding sincere people.

WELCOMING OTHER MINISTRY GIFTS

In the New Testament, Jesus gave ministry gifts to the Church:

"And he gave some, apostles; and some, prophets; and some, evangelists; and some, pastors and teachers."

— Ephesians 4:11

These ministry gifts were given to help equip and build up the body of Christ.

Different ministry gifts often carry different spiritual emphases. An evangelist often ministers in a way that stirs faith for salvation and healing. A prophet may bring revelation that gives clarity or direction. A teacher often establishes believers in truth.

These differences are not for rivalry. They are for supply.

We can understand this by thinking of skilled trades. Many people can do a little electrical work, a little carpentry, or a little plumbing around the house. But that does not make them an electrician, a carpenter, or a plumber by trade. A skilled tradesman has given himself to the knowledge of that work. He has experience in that work. He also has the proper tools to carry out that work.

Just as a carpenter or plumber has given himself to a particular trade, God-called ministers have given themselves to the work of the ministry. Through consecration, obedience, experience, and the grace of God, they carry knowledge and spiritual tools connected to their calling. Every member of the body is precious and necessary. But there are also those whom God has called, equipped, and set in the church to give themselves more fully to the work of ministry.

In a similar way, every believer can be used by God, and every believer may be led by the Spirit. But ministry gifts carry spiritual equipment suited to their office and calling.

This does not make one ministry gift better than another, and it does not make the minister greater than the body. It simply means that God has given different gifts for different functions, and the Church is helped when those gifts are received in their proper place.

Yet even when another ministry gift is present, the responsibility for shepherding the local congregation remains with the pastor. A visiting minister should be honored, but the local shepherd still carries responsibility for the house. Where there is mutual honor, both freedom and order are preserved.

It is wise for pastors to give visiting ministers clear expectations before the service. This does not restrict the Spirit. It preserves trust. A pastor may simply say:

"We welcome the move of the Spirit, and we want everything done in a way that strengthens the congregation and honors the order of this house."

TRAINING MATURE BELIEVERS

Mature believers also help sustain a healthy move of the Spirit by learning when to step forward and when to wait.

A Holy Ghost church needs people who are not only zealous, but teachable. Those who are often used in tongues, interpretation, prophecy, or other manifestations should be willing to receive guidance. They should not be offended by order. They should understand that the gift is not for personal display, but for the profit of the body.

Maturity is not proven by how quickly a person speaks. Sometimes it is proven by the ability to wait.

Pastors can help mature believers by giving private instruction, encouraging humility, and explaining the spiritual protocol of the house. This allows people to flow with the Spirit without opening the door to confusion.

A congregation grows healthier when spiritually sensitive people are also submitted, patient, and full of love.

PRACTICAL WAYS TO SHEPHERD THE FLOW

Pastors and leaders can make room for the Spirit in simple, practical ways.

They can teach regularly on the person and work of the Holy Ghost. They can explain the difference between private prayer in tongues and public utterance. They can allow quiet moments after worship without making the congregation feel pressured. They can give simple instruction before waiting on the Lord. They can encourage those who sense a tongue, interpretation, or prophecy to remain reverent, patient, and submitted to order.

They can also establish simple expectations. If someone is new to the church, or unsure how to respond to a prompting, that person can be encouraged to speak with leadership before moving publicly in spiritual utterance. This does not despise the gift. It helps preserve trust in the congregation.

The goal is not to make the service mechanical. The goal is to help the church become comfortable with the Spirit's moving in a way that is biblical, peaceful, and edifying.

A HEALTHY CHURCH

Leadership helps maintain clarity so that the congregation remains at peace. Mature believers help sustain a healthy move of the Spirit by learning how to yield in love and order. The congregation grows in confidence as it sees that the Holy Ghost can move without confusion.

In a healthy church, the Spirit is welcomed, Scripture guides the flow, and the body is strengthened.

The pastor does not control the Holy Ghost.

The pastor shepherds the house.

The people do not force spiritual manifestations.

The people remain yielded and ready.

The result is not disorder, fear, or confusion. The result is a church where the Word is honored, the Spirit is welcomed, and the people of God are edified.

CHAPTER 12

TONGUES AND INTERPRETATION: THE MINISTRY OF THE BODY

Among the manifestations of the Spirit, tongues with interpretation hold a unique place in the life of the church. Because they often involve more than one believer flowing together in the Spirit, they illustrate the theology of the body of Christ with special clarity.

By "the theology of the body of Christ," we simply mean that the body is not one member, but many. No believer stands alone. No one operates by himself. The members of the body need one another and function together for the good of the whole.

Paul includes both a tongue and an interpretation among the things that may be present when the church comes together:

"How is it then, brethren? when ye come together, every one of you hath a psalm, hath a doctrine, hath a tongue, hath a revelation, hath an interpretation. Let all things be done unto edifying."

— 1 Corinthians 14:26

For that reason, tongues with interpretation may rightly be

described as one of the crowning jewels of New Testament church life.

This operation of the Spirit is not centered on one personality. It is not dependent on a platform. It is the Spirit choosing to involve members of the body so that the whole congregation may be edified.

NOT PRIVATE PRAYER, BUT PUBLIC EDIFICATION

There is a difference between personal prayer in the Spirit and a tongue given in the gathered assembly. Tongues are supernatural utterance in both cases, but they serve different purposes. In private prayer, the believer speaks to God. In the public assembly, tongues with interpretation minister to men for the edification of the church.

In personal prayer, the believer speaks to God.

Paul said:

"For he that speaketh in an unknown tongue speaketh not unto men, but unto God..."

— 1 Corinthians 14:2

That is Godward. It is prayer. It is communion. It builds up the believer.

But when a tongue is given publicly in the gathered assembly, it is to be interpreted for the benefit of the congregation. Paul makes this clear when he says:

"But if there be no interpreter, let him keep silence in the church; and let him speak to himself, and to God."

— 1 Corinthians 14:28

That shows the public setting changes the order. If there is no interpreter, the believer may still speak to himself and to God, but the public message should wait until interpretation can bring understanding to the church.

The goal is always edification.

THE BODY WORKING TOGETHER

Tongues with interpretation often involve more than one believer. One yields to give the utterance. Another gives the interpretation. Both are responding to the same Spirit.

This is a beautiful picture of the body of Christ.

One member supplies what another does not. One speaks in a tongue. Another gives the interpretation. The congregation receives the benefit. The result is not individual display, but the strengthening of the whole body.

This does not mean it would be unscriptural for the same person to give both the tongue and the interpretation. Paul said:

"Wherefore let him that speaketh in an unknown tongue pray that he may interpret."

— 1 Corinthians 14:13

So Scripture allows for that possibility. But in a well-ordered church, this operation may involve more than one person. That is part of its beauty. It demonstrates that the Holy Ghost does not only work through one voice or one office. He ministers through the body.

A Holy Ghost church is not a spectator church. It is a body where believers are taught, yielded, and available to the Spirit.

INTERPRETATION BRINGS UNDERSTANDING

A tongue by itself does not edify the congregation unless it is interpreted. It may be a genuine utterance of the Spirit, but without interpretation the people do not understand what has been spoken.

Paul said:

"Except ye utter by the tongue words easy to be understood, how shall it be known what is spoken?"

— 1 Corinthians 14:9

This is why interpretation matters.

Interpretation is not a small addition to tongues. It is what allows the public utterance to profit the church. Through interpretation, what was unknown becomes understood, and the church is edified.

The interpretation does not have to sound dramatic to be spiritual. It does not have to be lengthy to be powerful. It simply needs to give the meaning of the utterance by the Spirit so that the congregation may receive edification.

THE TONGUE IS THE ORIGINAL UTTERANCE

It is important that we do not belittle the tongue itself.

Some have treated tongues as though they are only a strange introduction to the real message. Others have preferred to bypass tongues altogether and move directly into prophecy, as though interpretation were unnecessary if someone could simply speak prophetically in the known language.

But Paul did not treat tongues that way.

A public tongue is a legitimate manifestation of the Spirit. It is not empty sound. It is not spiritual decoration. It is not an inferior form of utterance. It is the original utterance given by the Spirit in a language unknown to the speaker and usually unknown to the congregation.

The interpretation follows so that the church may understand what has been spoken.

This is much like what happens when someone speaks in a foreign country through an interpreter. The original message is spoken first. The interpreter does not create a new message. He gives the meaning of what has already been said so that the hearers can understand and receive it.

In the same way, when a public tongue is given by the Spirit, the tongue itself carries the utterance. The interpretation brings that utterance into understandable form for the edifying of the church.

THE TONGUE HAS VALUE

Without interpretation, the congregation does not understand. But without the tongue, that particular manifestation has not been given. Tongues and interpretation work together. The interpretation does not make the tongue unnecessary. It reveals the meaning of the tongue so the church may be helped.

This is why Paul did not say, "Avoid tongues and only prophesy." He said, "forbid not to speak with tongues" (1 Corinthians 14:39), and he gave order for interpretation. The answer is not to set tongues aside, but to honor tongues and interpretation together in their proper place.

A Holy Ghost church should therefore not treat the public tongue as something to be endured until the interpretation comes. It should recognize the tongue as a true utterance of the Spirit and the interpretation as the God-given means by which that utterance profits the congregation.

REVELATION, KNOWLEDGE, PROPHECY, AND DOCTRINE

Paul gives an important insight:

"Except I shall speak to you either by revelation, or by knowledge, or by prophesying, or by doctrine..."

— 1 Corinthians 14:6

This verse shows the kind of edification that may come through tongues and interpretation.

When a tongue is interpreted, the message may bring revelation. It may bring knowledge. It may come in the manner of prophecy. It may communicate doctrine. However it comes, the purpose remains the same: the strengthening of the church.

This is one of the important truths at the heart of this book. Tongues and interpretation are not merely a sign that something spiritual has happened. They are one of the ways the Spirit of God may bring a present word to a present people.

A public tongue is not meant to end in mystery. It is meant to be interpreted so that the church can receive what the Spirit is saying.

NOT PERFORMANCE, BUT MINISTRY

Because tongues and interpretation are public, they must be handled with humility.

The person who gives the tongue is not performing. The person who interprets is not drawing attention to himself. He is serving the body by making the tongue understandable so the church may be edified.

Both are serving the body. The congregation is not there to admire the vessel, but to receive the ministry of the Spirit.

This keeps the operation pure.

No one should try to make the utterance impressive. No one should lengthen an interpretation for effect. No one should use a spiritual utterance to draw attention to himself. The Spirit of God does not manifest to exalt personality. He manifests to edify the Church and glorify Jesus.

When tongues and interpretation operate properly, the attention does not remain on the speaker. It turns the hearts of the people toward God.

THE CHURCH EDIFIED

Paul said:

"Greater is he that prophesieth than he that speaketh with tongues, except he interpret, that the church may receive edifying."

— 1 Corinthians 14:5

The phrase "except he interpret" is important. Tongues with interpretation brings public edification. In that sense, tongues and interpretation together become equivalent in benefit to prophecy because the church receives understanding.

This is why the operation should not be neglected. It is not unnecessary. It is one of the ways the Holy Ghost ministers to the gathered body.

When a tongue is given in order, and the interpretation follows by the Spirit, the congregation is strengthened. Faith rises. Hearts are encouraged. Direction may come. Comfort may be given. The presence of God is recognized among His people.

A PICTURE OF THE NEW TESTAMENT CHURCH

Tongues with interpretation reminds us that God delights to work through His people together.

One member yields.

Another member yields.

The whole body is edified.

It is a quiet picture of the Church functioning as God designed it.

The Spirit is not limited to the pulpit.

The congregation is not merely an audience.

The gifts are not for display.

The purpose is not confusion.

The Spirit speaks.

The body responds.

The Church is strengthened.

This is why tongues and interpretation belong in the gathered life of the local church. They show us the ministry of the body, the wisdom of divine order, and the goodness of God in giving supernatural help to His people.

PART III
THE GIFT OF TONGUES

"Wherefore, brethren, covet to prophesy, and forbid not to speak with tongues."
— 1 Corinthians 14:39

CHAPTER 13

THE PURPOSE OF TONGUES IN THE BELIEVER'S LIFE

If we are going to talk about tongues, we should begin with a simple truth: God does not give gifts to confuse His people. He gives gifts to help His people.

Speaking with other tongues is one of the ways the Holy Spirit strengthens the believer inwardly. It is not a badge. It is not a performance. It is not meant to make anyone look spiritual. It is a gift God gives so the believer can pray and worship beyond the limits of natural speech.

Paul said,

"For he that speaketh in an unknown tongue speaketh not unto men, but unto God: for no man understandeth him; howbeit in the spirit he speaketh mysteries."

— 1 Corinthians 14:2

Notice the direction: "unto God." Tongues are first Godward. They are a language of the spirit. They help us speak to God when our own words are insufficient.

This is why Jude wrote,

"But ye, beloved, building up yourselves on your most holy faith, praying in the Holy Ghost,"

—Jude 20

Praying in the Holy Ghost builds us up. It strengthens the believer and helps him remain steady. Many believers know what it is like to feel weak, tired, or worn down. Tongues are one of God's provisions for such moments. They help the believer pray when the mind is weary but the heart still reaches for God.

This does not mean we stop praying in our known language. Paul said:

"What is it then? I will pray with the spirit, and I will pray with the understanding also..."

— 1 Corinthians 14:15

We pray with the understanding, and we pray with the spirit. Both have their place. But tongues give the believer another stream of prayer and worship. It is the life of God at work within us.

PRIVATE PRAYER AND PUBLIC UNDERSTANDING

Paul gives us a clear balance:

"For if I pray in an unknown tongue, my spirit prayeth, but my understanding is unfruitful.

What is it then? I will pray with the spirit, and I will pray with the understanding also: I will sing with the spirit, and I will sing with the understanding also.

Else when thou shalt bless with the spirit, how shall he that occupieth the room of the unlearned say Amen at thy giving of thanks, seeing he understandeth not what thou sayest?

For thou verily givest thanks well, but the other is not edified.

I thank my God, I speak with tongues more than ye all:

Yet in the church I had rather speak five words with my understanding, that by my voice I might teach others also, than ten thousand words in an unknown tongue."

— 1 Corinthians 14:14–19

This passage is important because Paul does not correct tongues by despising tongues. He says, "I thank my God, I speak with tongues more than ye all." Paul valued tongues. He practiced tongues. He prayed in tongues abundantly.

Paul's words also show that praying in tongues is not passive or uncontrollable. He said, "I will pray with the spirit, and I will pray with the understanding also." The words "I will" show the believer's active cooperation. The Spirit supplies the utterance, but the believer chooses to yield, speak, pray, sing, continue, or stop. Tongues are supernatural, but they do not remove the believer's responsibility or self-control.

But Paul also understood the difference between private prayer and public ministry to the church. In private prayer, a believer may pray much in tongues and be personally strengthened. In the gathered assembly, when addressing the congregation, understanding must be present so the church can be edified.

That is why Paul said he would rather speak five words with understanding in the church than ten thousand words in an unknown tongue. He was not belittling tongues. He was teaching order. Tongues are Godward and profitable in the believer's prayer life. But when the church is being addressed, the people must receive understanding. If a tongue is given publicly, interpretation must follow so the body may be built up.

This balance protects both truths. We do not minimize praying in tongues, and we do not neglect understanding in the church. We pray with the spirit, and we pray with the understanding also. We sing with the spirit, and we sing with the understanding also.

PRAYER UNTO GOD

It is important to understand that not every use of tongues in a gathering is a public message to the congregation.

When a tongue is given as a public utterance addressed to the church, it should be interpreted so that the congregation may be edified. Paul is clear about that. But when believers are praying or worshiping together in the Spirit, the direction is Godward. They are not addressing the congregation. They are praying unto God.

This is why Paul said, "he that speaketh in an unknown tongue speaketh not unto men, but unto God" (1 Corinthians 14:2).

There may be times in a church service when believers pray together in the Spirit. There may be times of worship, intercession, or waiting upon the Lord when Spirit-filled believers lift their voices in tongues unto God. This does not have to be treated the same as a public message in tongues that calls for interpretation.

The purpose is different.

One is prayer unto God.

The other is utterance to the congregation.

Understanding this distinction helps remove confusion. It also helps believers become more comfortable with the gift of tongues in the public assembly.

STRENGTHENING THE BELIEVER

Praying in tongues strengthens the believer inwardly.

Paul said:

"He that speaketh in an unknown tongue edifieth himself..."

— 1 Corinthians 14:4

That does not mean selfishness. It means spiritual strengthening. The believer is built up. His spirit is strengthened. His heart is helped in prayer.

Every believer needs this kind of strengthening. There are times when the mind does not know what to say, but the spirit still reaches toward God. There are times when words in our own language feel too limited. There are times when the burden of prayer is deeper than our understanding.

In those moments, tongues are a gracious help from God.

They help us pray beyond the limitation of the mind, while still remaining in fellowship with God.

A HELP IN THE CONGREGATION

Although tongues strengthen the individual believer, their benefit does not remain individual only.

A Holy Ghost church is made up of Holy Ghost believers. When believers are strong on the inside, the church is stronger in its gathered life. A strengthened believer becomes a stronger part of the body of Christ.

For this reason, time taken in a service for prayer in the Spirit can be a great blessing when it is led wisely. It can help the congregation yield to God together. It can deepen the spirit of prayer. It can help believers become more familiar with how tongues operate in a church service.

It may also awaken the attention of the unbeliever or the

uninformed who may be present, provided it is handled with order, explanation, and wisdom.

A pastor may explain what is happening so visitors and younger believers are not confused. He may say something simple such as:

"We are going to take a moment to pray in the Spirit. If you are filled with the Holy Ghost, you may pray quietly and reverently in other tongues. We are not giving a public message to the congregation right now. We are praying unto God."

That kind of instruction brings peace. It allows Spirit-filled believers to pray, while also helping those unfamiliar with tongues understand what is taking place.

PERSONAL, BUT NOT PRIVATE ONLY

Tongues are personal, but they are not meant to be hidden away as though they are shameful.

They belong in the believer's daily walk with God. They also have a proper place in the gathered life of the church. The key is understanding the purpose and the setting.

In personal prayer, tongues build up the believer.

In corporate prayer, tongues may help the congregation pray together unto God.

In public utterance, tongues should be interpreted so the church may understand and be edified.

When these distinctions are taught clearly, confusion lessens and confidence grows.

In the chapters ahead, we will show more fully that tongues belong in the gathered church. But before we go there, we need to see that tongues were given for the believer's daily walk with God. They are a gift of fellowship, a gift of prayer, and a gift of spiritual strengthening.

CHAPTER 14

TONGUES IN PRAYER AND INTERCESSION

Many people think of tongues only in terms of a church service. But Scripture shows that tongues are also a prayer gift.

Sometimes we know exactly what to pray. At other times, we do not. We may know there is a need, but we cannot see the full picture. We may feel a burden, but we do not have the right words. In those moments, God has not left us helpless.

Paul wrote,

"Likewise the Spirit also helpeth our infirmities: for we know not what we should pray for as we ought: but the Spirit itself maketh intercession for us with groanings which cannot be uttered.

And he that searcheth the hearts knoweth what is the mind of the Spirit, because he maketh intercession for the saints according to the will of God.

And we know that all things work together for good to them that love God, to them who are the called according to his purpose."

— Romans 8:26–28

The Spirit "helpeth." He does not take over our responsibility, but He comes alongside us. He helps us pray when we do not know what to pray for as we ought.

This helps us understand why tongues are so valuable in the believer's prayer life. They help us pray beyond the limits of our own understanding while yielding to the help of the Holy Ghost.

This is not strange. It is God's gracious help.

THE HOLY SPIRIT HELPS US PRAY

When believers pray in tongues, they are cooperating with the Spirit of God who dwells within them. It is not about working up emotion. It is about yielding to the Spirit's help.

There are times when the mind does not know enough to pray accurately. We may only know part of a situation. We may not know the timing, the hidden need, the spiritual battle, or the full purpose of God. But the Spirit knows.

He knows the mind of God.

He knows the heart of man.

He knows the need better than we do.

We may not understand what we are saying, but we do know this: when we pray in the Holy Ghost, we position ourselves for divine help.

This also keeps us from spiritual pride. Tongues remind us that we do not know everything. They keep us dependent on God. They carry us beyond what the natural mind can understand.

Many believers can say, "I prayed in the Spirit, and later I understood why." At the moment of prayer, they did not have full knowledge. But the Spirit did.

PRAYER BEYOND NATURAL UNDERSTANDING

Paul said:

"For if I pray in an unknown tongue, my spirit prayeth, but my understanding is unfruitful."

— 1 Corinthians 14:14

This does not mean the prayer is unprofitable. It means the understanding does not grasp what is being prayed.

The mind may not understand, but the spirit is praying. That is why tongues are such a help in intercession. They allow the believer to pray when natural words are insufficient.

At times, a believer may sense a burden to pray and not know why. He may not have a name, a location, or a clear understanding of the situation. Yet as he prays in the Spirit, he is able to cooperate with the Holy Ghost.

This is one of God's appointed helps in prayer.

NOT A REPLACEMENT FOR THE WORD OR WISDOM

Tongues are not meant to replace the Word or replace wisdom. They are meant to help the believer pray and remain strong.

We still pray with understanding. We still ask God for wisdom. We still search the Scriptures. We still follow peace. Praying in tongues does not excuse foolishness or neglect of the Word.

But there are dimensions of prayer where natural understanding is limited. In those moments, the Spirit helps our infirmities.

The believer who prays in the Spirit is not abandoning

understanding. He is acknowledging that understanding alone is not enough.

CONTENDING FOR THE FAITH INCLUDES PRAYING IN THE HOLY GHOST

Jude wrote that believers should "earnestly contend for the faith which was once delivered unto the saints" (Jude 3).

That means the believer must not treat truth carelessly. We are called to hold fast to the faith, remain sound in doctrine, and guard what God has delivered to the Church.

In the same short epistle, Jude describes those who did not remain faithful. He says:

"These be they who separate themselves, sensual, having not the Spirit."

—Jude 19

That is a serious description. They were separated from the life and government of the Spirit. They were governed by the natural man, not by the Holy Ghost.

But Jude does not end with their error. In the very next verse, he turns to the believer and says:

"But ye, beloved, building up yourselves on your most holy faith, praying in the Holy Ghost,

Keep yourselves in the love of God, looking for the mercy of our Lord Jesus Christ unto eternal life."

—Jude 20–21

The contrast is important. Jude speaks of contending for the faith, warns about those who are sensual and have not the Spirit, and then says, "But ye, beloved." In other words, the beloved are not to follow the same course. They are to build themselves up on their most holy faith, praying in the Holy Ghost.

That does not mean praying in the Spirit replaces the Word

of God. It does not mean doctrine becomes unimportant. Sound doctrine must be built upon Scripture. But it does show us that praying in the Holy Ghost is one of God's appointed ways for believers to remain strong, guarded, and spiritually sound.

The Holy Ghost is the Spirit of truth. He is our Helper and Teacher. When a believer gives place to the Holy Ghost by praying in tongues, the Spirit helps him stay anchored in truth.

Praying in the Holy Ghost builds us up on our most holy faith. It helps keep us in the love of God. It helps keep the believer spiritually sensitive and steady, guarding the heart from drifting, dullness, and the weight of life's pressures.

When a believer prays in the Spirit, he is drawing from a gift God has given to strengthen his inner man.

THIS IS THE REST AND REFRESHING

Isaiah also spoke prophetically of this blessed gift of God:

"For with stammering lips and another tongue will he speak to this people.

To whom he said, This is the rest wherewith ye may cause the weary to rest; and this is the refreshing..."

— Isaiah 28:11–12

Isaiah called it rest and refreshing. When a believer prays in the Holy Ghost, he is receiving from the very provision God gave to strengthen and refresh His people.

Praying in the Holy Ghost does not make a believer careless with truth. It helps keep him strengthened in truth. It builds up the inward man, keeps the heart sensitive to God, and brings rest and refreshing to the weary soul.

CORPORATE PRAYER IN THE SPIRIT

This has application not only in private prayer, but also in the gathered church.

There may be times in a service when a pastor leads the congregation in prayer and invites Spirit-filled believers to pray in the Holy Ghost. This is not the same as a public message in tongues that requires interpretation. The direction is not from one person to the congregation. The direction is from the people unto God.

In such moments, the church may pray together in the Spirit. This can deepen intercession, strengthen the atmosphere of prayer, and help believers become more comfortable yielding to the Holy Ghost.

This should be done with wisdom and explanation, especially where people are unfamiliar with tongues. A pastor does not need to make the moment complicated. A simple explanation can bring peace and understanding.

That kind of instruction helps remove confusion. It teaches the people the difference between corporate prayer in the Spirit and a public tongue that needs interpretation.

Both have their place. Both should be handled in order. Both can strengthen the church.

A CHURCH PREPARED IN PRAYER

When a church is filled with believers who pray in the Spirit, that church is better prepared for the Spirit's moving when it gathers together.

Prayer in the Spirit helps cultivate sensitivity. It keeps believers spiritually active, focused, and yielded. It strengthens them on the inside so they are better prepared to respond to God, obey His Word, and do His work in practical ways.

A church that prays in the Holy Ghost will not be as easily satisfied with empty routine. Its people become more aware of God, more dependent on the Spirit, and more prepared for His direction.

This does not mean every service must look the same. It does not mean a congregation should force a certain pattern. But it does mean that prayer in the Spirit has a rightful place in the life of the believer and in the prayer life of the church.

The Holy Ghost helps us pray. God did not leave us to pray only with what we know. He gave us the Holy Ghost, help in our weakness, and a way to pray when we do not know what to pray for as we ought.

Tongues are a gift of prayer and intercession. They build up the believer and help him remain strong, dependent, sensitive, and spiritually alert.

In the next chapters, we will move from the believer's prayer life to the public life of the church, and we will show more fully how Scripture makes room for tongues and interpretation in the assembly.

CHAPTER 15

THE BEGINNING OF A SPIRIT-FILLED LIFE

When believers are filled with the Holy Spirit, it is natural to ask a simple question: How do we know it has happened?

God, in His kindness, did not leave the Church without an answer. Throughout the book of Acts, we are given a clear and repeated pattern that helps us understand what accompanied the infilling of the Spirit.

Again and again, when people were filled with the Holy Ghost, they spoke with other tongues.

This was not presented as something unusual. It was received as the normal outward expression of an inward experience.

THE PATTERN BEGINS AT PENTECOST

On the Day of Pentecost, the disciples were gathered together when the promise of the Father was fulfilled.

"And they were all filled with the Holy Ghost, and began to speak with other tongues, as the Spirit gave them utterance."

— Acts 2:4

Notice the simplicity of the verse.

They were filled.

They spoke.

The Spirit gave the utterance, but the believers gave the voice. From the beginning, speaking with tongues was connected to being filled with the Spirit.

THE PATTERN CONTINUES

As the gospel spread beyond Jerusalem, the same sign appeared.

When Peter preached at the house of Cornelius, something remarkable happened:

"While Peter yet spake these words, the Holy Ghost fell on all them which heard the word."

— Acts 10:44

How did those present recognize it?

"For they heard them speak with tongues, and magnify God."

— Acts 10:46

It was not a hidden experience. There was observable evidence.

Later, when Paul came to Ephesus, he asked a group of believers an important question:

"Have ye received the Holy Ghost since ye believed?"

— Acts 19:2

After laying hands on them:

"The Holy Ghost came on them; and they spake with tongues, and prophesied."

— Acts 19:6

Once again, the same pattern appears.

Filled with the Spirit.

Speaking with tongues.

When Scripture repeats something, it is inviting us to pay attention.

SALVATION AND THE INFILLING ARE NOT THE SAME

This is an important place for clarity.

At salvation, the Spirit baptizes the believer into the body of Christ. Paul writes:

"For by one Spirit are we all baptized into one body..."

— 1 Corinthians 12:13

But Jesus is the One who baptizes the believer with the Holy Ghost. John the Baptist declared:

"He shall baptize you with the Holy Ghost, and with fire."

— Matthew 3:11

Both works are beautiful.

Both are works of God.

Both are received by faith.

One brings us into Christ.

The other clothes us with power.

Understanding this distinction removes confusion and helps believers receive all that God desires to give.

THE SIGN OF A YIELDED TONGUE

Jesus said:

"And these signs shall follow them that believe; In my name shall they cast out devils; they shall speak with new tongues;"

— Mark 16:17

Speaking with new tongues is one of the signs Jesus said would follow believers. It should not be treated as strange, shameful, or out of place. It is a sign connected to the presence and power of the Holy Ghost.

James wrote:

"But the tongue can no man tame..."

—James 3:8

That makes this sign especially meaningful. Man cannot tame the tongue, but the believer can yield his tongue to the Holy Ghost.

When a believer speaks with other tongues, he is not trying to find the perfect words. He opens his mouth and speaks as the Spirit gives the utterance.

The member man cannot tame becomes the very member through which God gives supernatural utterance.

Speaking with tongues is the initial evidence of being filled with the Holy Ghost. The believer gives the voice, but the Spirit gives the utterance. The glory belongs to God, not to the vessel.

NOT FORCED, BUT RECEIVED

Speaking with tongues is never something a believer must struggle to produce. The Spirit gives the utterance. Our part is to yield in faith.

Just as salvation is received, the infilling of the Spirit is also received. God is not hesitant to give what He has promised.

Jesus said:

"If ye then, being evil, know how to give good gifts unto your children: how much more shall your heavenly Father give the Holy Spirit to them that ask him?"

— Luke 11:13

He is a willing giver.

The believer does not need to beg as though God were reluctant. He does not need to strain as though the experience depends on human effort. He asks, believes, receives, and yields to the utterance the Spirit gives.

The Spirit supplies.

The believer speaks.

A BEGINNING, NOT AN ENDING

It is important to understand that speaking with tongues is the beginning of a Spirit-filled life, not the goal.

God does not fill believers so they may merely say they had an experience. He fills them so they may live empowered lives, strengthened inwardly, sensitive to His leading, and ready to serve.

Tongues mark the beginning, but they are not the finish line. Beyond that beginning is a lifelong walk with the Spirit.

In the New Testament, tongues are more than an initial sign. They also become part of the believer's continuing life of prayer, worship, and yieldedness to God. This humble gift prepares the heart for deeper sensitivity and wider participation in the supernatural help God has provided for His Church.

That is one reason this gift has been so resisted and neglected. When believers neglect tongues, they may also become less open to other ways the Holy Ghost desires to help them. But when they receive this gift, honor it, and continue in it, they often become more open to the moving of the Holy Ghost in prayer, revelation, utterance, and spiritual power.

A GIFT FOR TODAY

The needs of the early Church have not disappeared. Believers still need strength. The Church still needs power to witness. The Church still depends on the help of the Spirit. It would be unlike

God to provide such a gift for one generation and quietly withdraw it from the next.

What He gave, He gave with foresight.

What He promised, He continues to supply.

The initial evidence of speaking with tongues is not the end of the Spirit-filled life. It is the beginning of a life of yieldedness, prayer, power, and greater sensitivity to the Holy Ghost.

CHAPTER 16

WHY TONGUES BELONG IN THE CHURCH

As we have seen, speaking with tongues strengthens the individual believer. Yet Scripture also reveals that this gift was never meant to remain only in private devotion. God intended for the life of the Spirit to touch the gathered church as well.

When we open the book of Acts, we do not find a church moving forward in its own strength. We find a church waiting for the promise of the Father. Jesus had told His disciples to tarry in Jerusalem until they were endued with power from on high. When the Holy Ghost was poured out, they were filled with power, given utterance, and sent forth as witnesses.

Paul's instructions to the Corinthians make this unmistakably clear:

"How is it then, brethren? when ye come together, every one of you hath a psalm, hath a doctrine, hath a tongue, hath a revelation, hath an interpretation. Let all things be done unto edifying."

— 1 Corinthians 14:26

Notice that a tongue is mentioned alongside worship, teaching, revelation, and interpretation. Paul was not describing something foreign to the gathered church. He was describing what could occur when believers came together.

The guiding principle was simple:

"Let all things be done unto edifying."

WHEN SILENCE REPLACES UNDERSTANDING

Sometimes churches grow cautious about the very things Scripture teaches us to desire. This does not always come from rebellion. Often, leaders are simply trying to preserve peace and protect the congregation.

Paul himself addressed misuse and confusion in Corinth. But it is important to see what he did not do. He did not forbid tongues. He brought order to them.

In fact, he concluded his teaching with these clear words:

"Wherefore, brethren, covet to prophesy, and forbid not to speak with tongues."

— 1 Corinthians 14:39

The instruction is both balanced and unmistakable. Desire what strengthens the church, and do not forbid what God has given.

A church should not allow abuse to drive it into disuse. The answer to misuse is not silence. The answer is understanding, order, and obedience to Scripture.

THE RIPPLE EFFECT OF ABSENCE

When a church makes little room for what Scripture permits, something subtle can happen over time.

Believers who might otherwise receive the baptism with the

Holy Ghost are never exposed to it. What is unfamiliar often feels unnecessary, and what feels unnecessary is rarely pursued.

Soon an entire generation may grow up sincerely loving God, yet unaware of the provision He intended for their strength and edification. This is rarely the result of deliberate resistance. More often, it is simply the result of silence.

But Scripture was given so the Church would not live beneath what God has supplied.

If tongues are never heard, never explained, never practiced, and never welcomed in any proper form, believers may begin to assume they have no real place in church life. But Paul did not write, "forbid not to speak with tongues" because tongues were to be hidden away. He wrote it because the Church needed to understand their place and keep them in order.

PUBLIC EXPRESSION AND THE LIFE OF THE CHURCH

It is helpful to remember that tongues may be expressed in more than one way within a gathering.

At times, believers may lift their voices to God in the Spirit, speaking with tongues in worship, prayer, or praise. In such moments, the focus is Godward. This is not a public message being addressed to the congregation. It is prayer or worship unto God.

Paul said:

"For he that speaketh in an unknown tongue speaketh not unto men, but unto God..."

— 1 Corinthians 14:2

Because the direction is Godward, this kind of praying or worshiping in tongues does not require interpretation in the same way a public message in tongues does.

At other times, a tongue may be given publicly to the congregation. In that case, it should be interpreted so that all may be edified.

These two expressions should not be confused.

One is prayer unto God.

The other is utterance to the congregation.

Both have their place. Both can be handled with order. Both can contribute to the spiritual life of the church when guided by Scripture.

MAKING ROOM WITHOUT CONFUSION

A pastor can bring clarity with a few simple instructions. This can remove confusion, help visitors feel at ease, and help younger believers understand the difference between prayer in the Spirit and a public tongue requiring interpretation.

If the church is entering a time of corporate prayer in the Spirit, the pastor can explain that the people are praying unto God, not giving a message to the congregation.

If the church is waiting for a public tongue and interpretation, the pastor can explain that the congregation will wait for the interpretation so the church may be edified.

The goal is not to force tongues into a service. The goal is to make sure the church does not crowd out what Scripture allows and encourages.

NOT FEAR, BUT UNDERSTANDING

Some hesitation surrounding public expression has come from a sincere desire to avoid disorder. That concern is understandable. No shepherd wants confusion among the people he serves.

Yet the answer to misuse has never been removal. It has always been understanding.

Paul did not write to the Corinthians to silence spiritual expression. He wrote so that it would bless rather than distract. Where Scripture guides, fear begins to loosen its hold.

A church does not have to choose between liberty and order. The same Bible that says, "forbid not to speak with tongues," also says, "Let all things be done decently and in order."

A church can pray in the Spirit without becoming disorderly. It can allow tongues with interpretation without creating confusion. It can make room for spiritual utterance while still keeping the service understandable and edifying.

That is not compromise. That is New Testament order.

A SIGN TO THE UNBELIEVER

Paul also speaks of the effect tongues may have on those unfamiliar with the ways of God:

"Wherefore tongues are for a sign, not to them that believe, but to them that believe not..."

— 1 Corinthians 14:22

This reminds us that the Spirit's work often reaches further than we can see. God knows how to use what He has given to draw attention to His presence.

At the same time, Paul also made clear that the church must handle spiritual utterance with wisdom and order. If tongues are misunderstood or disorderly, the unlearned may become confused. That is why teaching and order matter.

Even on the Day of Pentecost, people responded in different ways. Some were amazed. Some doubted. Others mocked and said, "These men are full of new wine."

— Acts 2:12–13

But Peter did not hide what had happened. He explained it from Scripture:

"But this is that which was spoken by the prophet Joel;"

— Acts 2:16

That gives the Church a wise pattern. When people do not understand the work of the Spirit, the answer is not embarrassment or silence. The answer is clear, scriptural explanation.

The fact that some people misunderstand tongues does not mean tongues are wrong. It means people need instruction.

The church cannot force these moments, but it can make room for them in a way that remains open to the Spirit and governed by the Word.

When an unbeliever or uninformed person hears believers praying in the Spirit, or hears a public tongue followed by interpretation, he may recognize that something beyond mere human speech is taking place. That does not mean every visitor will immediately understand everything. The possibility of misunderstanding should not cause the Church to forbid tongues. Scripture presents tongues as a sign following believers and also as a sign to unbelievers.

The answer is not to hide the gift.

The answer is to handle the gift scripturally.

RESTORING WHAT WAS ALWAYS MEANT TO BE

A Holy Ghost church is not striving to become unusual. It is simply returning to the pattern Scripture reveals.

When leadership teaches clearly, believers understand, and order is honored, the church discovers that spiritual expression need not feel disruptive. Instead, it becomes part of a healthy rhythm of worship, prayer, teaching, and ministry.

The result is not confusion.

It is life.

A church may take time for corporate prayer in the Spirit.

It may wait quietly for tongues and interpretation.

It may teach believers how to respond.

It may help visitors understand what is happening.

It may give place to spiritual utterance without surrendering order.

These are not strange additions to church life. They are part of the Spirit-filled life of the body.

A QUIET INVITATION

Perhaps the safest way forward is neither force nor neglect, but gentle openness. A church does not have to rush into anything unfamiliar. Yet it should remain willing to embrace what the Word makes available.

God has not withdrawn His gifts.

He has not changed His mind about the Spirit-filled church.

What He gave to the early Church, He still desires to work among His people today.

A Holy Ghost church does not have to be confused, careless, or disorderly. It can be Word-honoring, Spirit-filled, peaceful, and alive.

It can make room for tongues.

It can make room for interpretation.

It can make room for the Holy Ghost.

CHAPTER 17

UNDERSTANDING PAUL'S INSTRUCTIONS

Whenever God gives something precious to His Church, He also provides the wisdom needed to steward it well. Spiritual expressions were never meant to create uncertainty among believers. Through the apostle Paul, the Lord gave clear guidance so that the life of the Spirit could flourish in an atmosphere of peace.

Paul's words were not written to restrain the Church, but to steady it. When we understand what he was saying, and why he was saying it, much of the concern surrounding spiritual manifestations begins to fade.

WHEN YOU COME TOGETHER

Paul writes:

"How is it then, brethren? when ye come together, every one of you hath a psalm, hath a doctrine, hath a tongue, hath a revelation, hath an interpretation. Let all things be done unto edifying."

— 1 Corinthians 14:26

Notice the setting: "when ye come together."

Paul expected the gathering of believers to be participatory. Worship had a place. Teaching had a place. Tongues, revelation, and interpretation also had a place. The service was not to be careless or disorderly, but neither was it to be so controlled that the members of the body had no room to function.

Yet over all of it he placed one guiding principle:

"Let all things be done unto edifying."

The question is never merely, "Did something spiritual happen?" The question is, "Did it strengthen the church?"

Edification is the compass.

ORDER, NOT SUPPRESSION

Paul continues:

"If any man speak in an unknown tongue, let it be by two, or at the most by three, and that by course; and let one interpret."

— 1 Corinthians 14:27

Paul is not suppressing spiritual utterance. He is showing the church how it is to operate in order.

"Two, or at the most by three" shows that spiritual expression was never meant to dominate a service. It was meant to contribute to the strengthening of the body without overwhelming the gathering.

"And that by course" means one at a time. The Spirit does not produce confusion by prompting many voices to compete with one another. When believers understand this, they learn the quiet wisdom of waiting.

Sometimes the most spiritual thing a person can do is pause. Yieldedness includes patience.

LET ONE INTERPRET

Paul also says, "and let one interpret."

A public tongue is not meant to remain a mystery to the congregation. If it is given publicly, it should be interpreted so the church may receive understanding and edification.

This does not mean it would be unscriptural for the same person to give the tongue and also interpret. Paul plainly says:

"Wherefore let him that speaketh in an unknown tongue pray that he may interpret."

— 1 Corinthians 14:13

So Scripture leaves room for that possibility. Yet in a well-ordered church, it is wise to honor the pattern and leadership of the local assembly. Spiritual freedom and spiritual order were never meant to compete. In a healthy church, they work together.

Public utterance is not merely a matter of ability. It is also a matter of order, timing, interpretation, and edification.

IF THERE IS NO INTERPRETER

Paul then gives what may be one of the most misunderstood instructions:

"But if there be no interpreter, let him keep silence in the church; and let him speak to himself, and to God."

— 1 Corinthians 14:28

Notice carefully that Paul does not forbid the believer from speaking altogether. Instead, he redirects the expression.

There is still communion with God.

There is still prayer.

There is still spiritual life.

But the public message waits until interpretation can bring

understanding to all. This protects the congregation from confusion while honoring the work of the Spirit.

THE SPIRIT LEADS, HE DOES NOT DRIVE

Further into the chapter, Paul gives a statement that has steadied countless leaders:

"And the spirits of the prophets are subject to the prophets."

— 1 Corinthians 14:32

Simply put, spiritual influence does not remove personal responsibility. A believer is never overtaken in such a way that self-control disappears.

The Spirit leads.

He does not drive.

This truth alone answers many quiet fears. The presence of the Spirit does not produce chaos. It produces clarity within yielded hearts.

A person can wait.

A person can yield.

A person can speak in order.

A person can remain silent when order requires it.

That is not resisting the Spirit. That is cooperating with Him according to the Word.

GOD IS THE AUTHOR OF PEACE

Paul then anchors everything with these words:

"For God is not the author of confusion, but of peace, as in all churches of the saints."

— 1 Corinthians 14:33

Where God is truly welcomed, peace will be present.

Not stiffness.

Not heaviness.

Peace.

A church never has to choose between spiritual life and stability. Scripture shows us that both can exist together beautifully.

The Spirit gives life.

The Word gives instruction.

Together, they produce peace and order.

WHAT PAUL WAS REALLY DOING

It is important to remember that Paul was writing to a church rich in spiritual activity but lacking maturity in how that activity was expressed. His goal was not to silence them. His goal was to help them grow.

Correction, when it comes from love, is never meant to diminish. It is meant to strengthen.

Paul saw what the Corinthians were experiencing and, in essence, said: This is good; now let us bring understanding so it blesses everyone.

That remains wise counsel for the Church today.

FREEDOM WITHIN ORDER

Some have feared that structure might hinder the Spirit. Yet Scripture reveals the opposite. Order does not quench the Spirit. It protects what He desires to do.

Think of riverbanks guiding a flowing river. Without them, the water spreads and loses strength. With them, it moves with purpose.

Order is not limitation.

It is guidance.

The purpose of order is not to stop the river. The purpose of order is to help the river flow in a way that brings life.

A CHURCH AT REST

When leadership understands Paul's instructions and teaches them clearly, something beautiful begins to happen within a congregation: people relax.

They no longer fear that spiritual moments will become disruptive. Instead, they learn to recognize the gentle leadership of the Spirit and trust the biblical framework that surrounds it.

Confidence grows.

Hunger grows.

Expectation grows.

And the church begins to function with both life and peace.

This is what Paul's instructions make possible: not a silent church, not a careless church, but a Spirit-filled church where the Holy Ghost is welcomed, the Word is honored, and the body is edified.

CHAPTER 18

"WHEN YE COME TOGETHER": MAKING ROOM FOR TONGUES AND INTERPRETATION

Paul did not treat tongues and interpretation as optional extras. In 1 Corinthians 14, he speaks of these things as part of the gathered church.

He wrote:

"How is it then, brethren? when ye come together, every one of you hath a psalm, hath a doctrine, hath a tongue, hath a revelation, hath an interpretation. Let all things be done unto edifying."

— 1 Corinthians 14:26

Notice the setting: "when ye come together."

Paul is not speaking only of private devotion. He is speaking of the gathered assembly. He mentions a psalm, a doctrine, a tongue, a revelation, and an interpretation, then gives the governing principle: "Let all things be done unto edifying."

Most churches understand a psalm and a doctrine. Singing and preaching are expected. But many have treated a tongue and an interpretation as though they were rare, risky, or unnecessary.

Paul did not speak that way.

If a church left out singing week after week, people would notice. If a church never preached, people would complain. Yet many churches have left out tongues and interpretation for years, and some have come to accept that as normal.

But that is not the New Testament pattern.

THE MISSING INGREDIENT

Think of it like a recipe. If one ingredient is left out, something may still be produced, but it will not be exactly what it was meant to be.

In the same way, many believers have never experienced what it is like for a church service to include all the elements Paul listed. They have never seen tongues and interpretation function in a steady, peaceful way. They have never heard an utterance given by the Spirit for the edifying of the church.

They may love God.

They may love the Word.

They may be sincere and faithful.

But they may still be living without something God intended to help the Church.

ORDER MAKES ROOM POSSIBLE

Paul does not merely tell us that a tongue and interpretation may be present. He also gives the order:

"If any man speak in an unknown tongue, let it be by two, or at the most by three, and that by course; and let one interpret."

— 1 Corinthians 14:27

This is not chaos. This is order.

Then he tells us what to do if there is no interpreter:

"But if there be no interpreter, let him keep silence in the church; and let him speak to himself, and to God."

— 1 Corinthians 14:28

That verse matters. It protects the church. It protects the move of the Spirit. It keeps things from becoming confusing.

It also shows that tongues are not being shut down. The person may still speak to himself and to God. But in the public setting, interpretation is required if the whole body is to be edified.

Order does not remove tongues from the church. Order makes room for tongues to function properly in the church.

MORE THAN BELIEVING IN THEORY

This means leadership must do more than believe in tongues. Leadership must make room for them in the service.

A church may believe in tongues doctrinally and yet never allow a practical place for tongues and interpretation to operate. If every service is so full, so hurried, or so tightly arranged that there is no moment to wait upon the Lord, then what is believed on paper may never be experienced in the congregation.

There is no Scripture that says tongues and interpretation must happen during singing, after singing, before the sermon, or after the message. The Bible gives order, but it does not lock every church into one placement.

That is where wise leadership comes in.

A pastor may choose a quiet moment after worship, during prayer, or before the preaching of the Word. The exact placement may vary from service to service. The issue is not the exact point in the service, but whether the Holy Ghost is given room to minister.

If space is not given, these things will rarely function in the gathered assembly.

CREATING A CLEAR MOMENT

A pastor can help the congregation by creating a clear moment.

He may say:

"Let us wait before the Lord for a moment. We are not trying to force anything. We simply want to give room for the Holy Ghost to minister as He wills."

Or he may say:

"If the Spirit gives a public tongue, we will wait for the interpretation so that the church may be edified."

Or he may say:

"We want everything done in peace and order. If you are unsure how to respond, wait and remain sensitive to the Lord."

Such language does not have to be used every time, but it can help a congregation learn. It removes pressure. It prevents awkwardness. It teaches the people how to recognize the difference between a general time of prayer and a public utterance that needs interpretation.

A church that is learning these things needs clear, calm leadership.

AN UTTERANCE GIVEN BY THE SPIRIT

When tongues and interpretation operate properly, the church receives more than a spiritual moment. It receives the ministry of the Holy Ghost.

The message may bring comfort. It may bring exhortation. It may bring revelation. It may bring knowledge. It may stir faith. It may call the church to respond to God.

However it comes, the purpose is always edification.

This is why tongues and interpretation should not be treated as unnecessary. They are one of the ways the Spirit of God may bring an utterance for the edifying of the church.

The church does not need to manufacture that utterance. It simply needs to make room for the Spirit to give it.

MAKING ROOM FOR TONGUES AND INTERPRETATION

A Holy Ghost church does not merely allow the Spirit in theory. It makes room for the Spirit in practice.

It teaches believers what Scripture says.

It explains the difference between private prayer and public utterance.

It gives room to wait upon the Lord.

It keeps order without fear.

It honors interpretation when a public tongue is given.

It refuses to forbid what Scripture says not to forbid.

This is not complicated, but it must be intentional.

A church will rarely drift into a healthy operation of tongues and interpretation by accident. It must be taught, shepherded, and given room.

THE NEW TESTAMENT PATTERN

The New Testament pattern is not a silent church. It is not a careless church either.

It is a church where worship, doctrine, revelation, tongues, and interpretation may all serve the edification of the body.

A Holy Ghost church does not need to become strange. It needs to become scriptural.

It does not need to force manifestations.

It needs to make room.

It does not need to abandon order.

It needs to obey order.

It does not need to fear tongues and interpretation.

It needs to understand them, welcome them, and allow them to function as the Spirit wills.

When the church comes together, the Holy Ghost should not be crowded out of His own house.

CHAPTER 19

ORDER AMONG LEADERS: "LET THE PROPHETS SPEAK"

Paul's instructions in 1 Corinthians 14 are not only about tongues. He also speaks about prophecy and order among those ministering in the service.

"Let the prophets speak two or three, and let the other judge.

If any thing be revealed to another that sitteth by, let the first hold his peace.

For ye may all prophesy one by one, that all may learn, and all may be comforted.

And the spirits of the prophets are subject to the prophets.

For God is not the author of confusion, but of peace, as in all churches of the saints."

— 1 Corinthians 14:29–33

This passage has often been misunderstood. Some read, "ye may all prophesy," and imagine a whole congregation lining up to prophesy one by one. That is not what Paul is describing.

In context, Paul is speaking about order among those ministering prophetically in the meeting. He says, "Let the prophets speak two or three." That sets the frame. He is describing how prophetic utterance is to function when the church is gathered.

The instruction is not open-ended disorder. It is ordered participation.

TWO OR THREE

Paul says, "Let the prophets speak two or three."

That phrase immediately gives boundaries. Prophetic utterance should not take over the whole service. It should serve the purpose of God in the meeting and strengthen the body.

This is similar to Paul's instruction concerning tongues. He allows room for spiritual utterance, but he does not allow it to become excessive or confusing.

God is not wasteful.

He is purposeful.

The goal is not for everyone to say something. The goal is for the church to be edified.

LET THE OTHER JUDGE

Paul also says, "let the other judge."

Prophecy is not to be despised, but neither is it to be received carelessly. It is to be weighed.

Judging does not mean harsh criticism. It means mature spiritual evaluation. What is spoken should be measured by the Word of God, by the witness of the Spirit, and by the oversight of those responsible for the service.

This keeps the church safe without shutting down the Spirit.

A church should not be gullible.

A church should not be cynical.

It should be spiritual.

LET THE FIRST HOLD HIS PEACE

Paul continues:

"If any thing be revealed to another that sitteth by, let the first hold his peace."

There is a spirit behind this instruction: humility.

Do not compete.

Do not push.

Do not act as though you must dominate the service.

If another receives something by the Spirit, the first can hold his peace. That requires humility and trust. It shows that the vessel is not more important than the message, and the message is not more important than the edification of the body.

A person who is truly yielded to the Spirit does not have to fight for attention.

ONE BY ONE

Paul says, "For ye may all prophesy one by one, that all may learn, and all may be comforted."

The phrase "one by one" matters.

The Spirit does not require confusion in order to manifest. He does not need people speaking over one another. He does not need pressure, competition, or haste.

One by one means the congregation can hear.

One by one means the message can be weighed.

One by one means the church can receive comfort and instruction.

Order allows the gift to accomplish its purpose.

THE SPIRITS OF THE PROPHETS

Then Paul gives one of the most stabilizing truths in the whole discussion:

"And the spirits of the prophets are subject to the prophets."

That means self-control is present. People do not have to interrupt everything. They can wait. They can yield. They can be led. They can be taught.

Spiritual influence does not remove responsibility.

The Spirit leads.

He does not drive.

This is one reason many pastors have drawn back after witnessing disorder. They have seen people act as though they could not control themselves, and they concluded that the only safe answer was silence.

But Paul shows a better answer.

The answer is not silence.

The answer is Scripture-governed order.

GOD IS THE AUTHOR OF PEACE

Paul gives the reason:

"For God is not the author of confusion, but of peace, as in all churches of the saints."

Peace is not the absence of the gifts. Peace is the fruit of the gifts being stewarded well.

A church can have prophecy and peace.

A church can have tongues and interpretation and peace.

A church can have revelation and peace.

A church can have the moving of the Spirit and peace.

Disorder is not a mark of spirituality, and deadness is not a sign of peace. In a Holy Ghost church, the Spirit is welcomed and the Word governs the flow.

A STEADY ATMOSPHERE

This kind of order creates a steady atmosphere in the church.

Leadership does not have to fear spiritual manifestations. Believers do not have to feel pressure to perform. Those who are used by the Spirit learn to move with humility, patience, and reverence.

The service remains steady.

The people remain at peace.

The Spirit is not quenched.

The body is edified.

As we move forward, we will continue to see how leadership can cultivate this kind of atmosphere, where the Spirit is welcomed, the service is steady, and manifestations can occur without fear.

CHAPTER 20

"AS HE WILL": SOVEREIGNTY WITHOUT EXCUSES

There is a verse many people quote when the gifts of the Spirit are discussed:

"But all these worketh that one and the selfsame Spirit, dividing to every man severally as he will."

— 1 Corinthians 12:11

That is true. The Spirit of God is sovereign. The gifts are not controlled by human planning, human desire, or human effort. No one can manufacture a move of God.

But some have used this verse to justify passivity. They reason that if the Spirit divides as He wills, then believers should simply wait and do nothing. But Paul never used the sovereignty of the Spirit to cancel the responsibility of the Church.

That is not how Paul teaches.

The same apostle who wrote 1 Corinthians 12 also wrote 1 Corinthians 14. In chapter 12, he tells us that the Spirit divides as He wills. In chapter 14, he gives clear instructions about what to do when believers come together.

That tells us something important: the Spirit's sovereignty is not an excuse for the Church's passivity.

The Spirit is sovereign.

The Word is clear.

The Church is responsible to obey.

WE CANNOT FORCE, BUT WE CAN MAKE ROOM

A church cannot force manifestations, but it can remove barriers. It can teach the Word, prepare hearts, make room in the service, encourage believers to desire spiritual gifts, obey the order Scripture gives, and refuse to forbid what God has provided.

None of that controls the Spirit. It simply brings the church into cooperation with the Word.

There is a difference between trying to make something happen and making room for what God desires to do. One is presumption. The other is obedience.

A Holy Ghost church does not say, "The Spirit divides as He wills," and then make no room for Him to move. It honors His sovereignty by obeying His Word.

MIXED REACTIONS ARE NOT AN EXCUSE

As we saw from the Day of Pentecost, people do not always respond to the move of the Spirit in the same way. When the multitude heard the believers speaking with tongues, some were amazed, some wondered, and others mocked.

"And they were all amazed, and were in doubt, saying one to another, What meaneth this?

Others mocking said, These men are full of new wine."

— Acts 2:12–13

But mixed reactions were not a reason to retreat. Peter did not hide what God had done. He did not apologize for the manifestation of the Spirit. He stood up and explained it from Scripture.

"But Peter, standing up with the eleven, lifted up his voice, and said unto them... For these are not drunken, as ye suppose, seeing it is but the third hour of the day.

But this is that which was spoken by the prophet Joel;"

— Acts 2:14–16

That is important. Peter did not treat misunderstanding as a reason to shut down what God had done. He answered confusion with Scripture. He showed the people that what they were seeing was not drunkenness, emotional excess, or disorder. It was the fulfillment of what God had spoken by the prophet Joel.

That remains a wise pattern for leaders today. When the Spirit moves and people do not understand, leaders should not panic, hide, or apologize. They should teach. They should explain. They should anchor the people in the Word.

Mixed reactions are not a reason to eliminate tongues. They are a reason to teach and lead well.

TONGUES AS A SIGN

Paul also says plainly:

"Wherefore tongues are for a sign, not to them that believe, but to them that believe not..."

— 1 Corinthians 14:22

That does not mean every unbeliever will respond in the same way. Acts 2 proves that. Some were amazed. Some were in doubt. Others mocked. But mixed reactions did not cancel the sign.

Tongues remain a public witness that something beyond the natural is present among God's people. They testify that God is living, active, and working in His Church.

This helps us understand Paul's warning in 1 Corinthians 14. If the whole church comes together and all speak with tongues without order or interpretation, the unbeliever or unlearned may say, "Ye are mad" (1 Corinthians 14:23). But the answer is not to forbid tongues. The answer is to handle tongues according to Scripture, with interpretation, order, and edification.

A sign is not given because everyone already understands it. A sign is given because God desires to arrest attention and bear witness to His presence.

This does not mean tongues should be handled carelessly. Paul still gives order. He still requires interpretation for a public message in tongues. He still teaches that all things should be done unto edifying.

But the possibility of misunderstanding does not give us permission to remove what Scripture calls a sign.

TEACHING ANSWERS CONFUSION

If people are unfamiliar with tongues, the answer is teaching.

If visitors do not understand what is happening, the answer is explanation.

If believers are uncertain, the answer is patient instruction.

On the Day of Pentecost, Peter did not leave the people to guess what was happening. He explained the moment from Scripture. He said, "This is that which was spoken by the prophet Joel" (Acts 2:16).

That remains a pattern for leaders today.

A Holy Ghost church does not hide the Spirit's work because

some may misunderstand. It teaches so misunderstanding can give way to faith.

TWO TRUTHS TOGETHER

We must keep two truths together:

- - The Spirit divides as He wills.
- - The Church obeys the Word and makes room.

If we only emphasize the Spirit's sovereignty, we may become passive. If we only emphasize the Church's responsibility, we may become pressured or performative. Scripture gives us the balance.

We do not manufacture.
We do not retreat.
We do not force.
We do not forbid.
We do not control the Spirit.
We obey the Word.
That is the safe place.

THE NEW TESTAMENT PATTERN

We are not trying to recreate another generation's experience. We are not trying to imitate a style, a personality, or a former move of God.

We are trying to follow the New Testament pattern with peace and order.

That pattern includes the Spirit distributing as He wills. It also includes believers desiring spiritual gifts. It includes tongues as a sign. It includes interpretation for public edification. It includes leadership teaching and shepherding the congregation. It includes order that protects the move of the Spirit rather than shutting it down.

This is what wise shepherding looks like.

The Spirit is sovereign.

The Church is responsible.

The Word gives order.

The people make room.

And when those truths are kept together, the Church can welcome the Holy Ghost without fear, without pressure, and without excuse.

CHAPTER 21

TONGUES, PROPHECY, AND THE UNBELIEVER

Paul also deals with the effect of tongues and prophecy upon the unbeliever and the unlearned. He writes:

"In the law it is written, With men of other tongues and other lips will I speak unto this people; and yet for all that will they not hear me, saith the Lord.

Wherefore tongues are for a sign, not to them that believe, but to them that believe not: but prophesying serveth not for them that believe not, but for them which believe.

If therefore the whole church be come together into one place, and all speak with tongues, and there come in those that are unlearned, or unbelievers, will they not say that ye are mad?

But if all prophesy, and there come in one that believeth not, or one unlearned, he is convinced of all, he is judged of all:

And thus are the secrets of his heart made manifest; and so falling down on his face he will worship God, and report that God is in you of a truth."

— 1 Corinthians 14:21–25

A SIGN SOME WOULD NOT HEAR

Paul is referring back to Isaiah's words:

"For with stammering lips and another tongue will he speak to this people."

— Isaiah 28:11

Isaiah's prophecy continues with this sober statement:

"Yet they would not hear."

— Isaiah 28:12

That phrase is important. It shows that God may give a sign, and yet some may still refuse to hear. The fact that some people misunderstand, mock, or reject a manifestation does not prove the manifestation is wrong. It proves that not every heart will receive what God is doing.

MISUNDERSTANDING IS NOT A REASON TO REMOVE TONGUES

We see this clearly on the Day of Pentecost. When the Holy Ghost was poured out and the disciples began to speak with other tongues, the response was mixed. Some were amazed. Some were in doubt. Others mocked and said, "These men are full of new wine" (Acts 2:4, 12–13). But Peter did not apologize for the manifestation, and he did not shut it down. Instead, he stood up and explained from the Scriptures what was taking place (Acts 2:14–16).

That is an important pattern. When spiritual things are misunderstood, the answer is not to deny the Spirit's work. The answer is to bring scriptural explanation.

Paul says tongues are for a sign to them that believe not. That means tongues have sign value. They bear witness that something supernatural is taking place among God's people. But

Paul also warns that if the whole church comes together and all speak with tongues without order or interpretation, the unlearned or unbeliever may say, "Ye are mad."

The problem is not tongues themselves. The problem is tongues without understanding in the gathered assembly.

This is where many churches have drawn the wrong conclusion. They have assumed that because someone may misunderstand tongues, tongues should be removed from the church. But Paul does not say that. He does not say, "Forbid tongues so no one is uncomfortable." He says, "forbid not to speak with tongues," and then he gives order for their proper operation.

The possibility of misunderstanding is not a reason to remove what God has given. It is a reason to teach, interpret, explain, and keep all things in order.

Many things in the Gospel are misunderstood by the natural mind. The cross itself is foolishness to them that perish, yet we do not stop preaching Christ crucified. The virgin birth is rejected by many, yet we do not remove it from our doctrine. The resurrection is mocked by unbelievers, yet we do not soften it to make it easier for the natural mind to receive.

In the same way, we must not remove tongues, interpretation, prophecy, or the manifestations of the Spirit simply because some may not understand them at first. We teach. We explain. We interpret when interpretation is required. We keep order. But we do not remove from the Church what God has placed in the Church.

TONGUES, PROPHECY, AND UNDERSTANDING

Then Paul shows the effect of prophecy. If the unbeliever or unlearned person comes in and the secrets of his heart are made manifest, he may fall down and worship God, declaring that God is truly among the people.

This shows us that tongues and prophecy both have a place, but they do not function in exactly the same way. Tongues may serve as a sign. Prophecy brings understanding, conviction, and edification in a known language. Tongues with interpretation brings understanding to the church. In all of this, the goal remains the same: God is revealed, Christ is honored, and the people are helped.

A Holy Ghost church does not hide the supernatural because unbelievers may be present. Neither does it ignore order because believers are present. It welcomes the Spirit in such a way that both the believer and the unbeliever may recognize that God is truly among His people.

After all of Paul's instruction, he closes with words that are simple and strong:

"Wherefore, brethren, covet to prophesy, and forbid not to speak with tongues."

— 1 Corinthians 14:39

Paul did not spend a whole chapter teaching order so the Church would avoid tongues. He taught order so the Church could embrace tongues without confusion.

Then he adds:

"Let all things be done decently and in order."

— 1 Corinthians 14:40

These two verses belong together. Paul says, "forbid not," and then he says, "let all things be done decently and in order." He does not set liberty against order. He brings them together.

Not silence, but order.

Not fear, but peace.

Not retreat, but obedience.

The Church must not forbid what God has given. At the

same time, it must not handle holy things carelessly. Tongues are to be welcomed, taught, interpreted when given publicly, and governed by the Word.

WHY THIS MATTERS

If we forbid what God has given, we lose part of the life He intended for His Church. We may still have singing. We may still have preaching. We may still have organization and activity. But we will be living beneath the New Testament pattern.

Tongues belong in the believer's life.

Tongues belong in prayer.

Tongues belong in worship and intercession.

Tongues belong in the church when interpretation is present.

And Scripture plainly says, "forbid not to speak with tongues."

That should settle something in our hearts.

The answer to misuse is not disuse. The answer to confusion is not silence. The answer is understanding, faith, order, and obedience.

MAKING ROOM WITHOUT FORCING

At the same time, we remember that the Spirit is sovereign. He distributes as He wills.

We do not try to control Him.

We do not try to manufacture His work.

We do not try to produce a manifestation by human effort.

But we do make room.

We do prepare.

We do teach.

We do take time to explain when the unlearned or unbelievers are present.

We do desire spiritual gifts.

We do obey the order Scripture gives.

And when God moves, we do not panic. We do not shut it down. We steward it in peace.

A Holy Ghost church is not a church that tries to force spiritual activity. It is a church that refuses to crowd out the Spirit's activity.

IT CAN HAPPEN

Many believers have never been in a service where tongues and interpretation function in a steady, biblical way. They have never seen how simple it can be when leadership is wise, the people are taught, and the Word is honored.

But it can happen.

A message in tongues should be given in peace and order, not force or frenzy.

An interpretation can follow with clarity.

The church can receive edification.

The congregation can remain at rest.

Visitors can be helped by simple explanation.

Leaders can guide without fear.

Believers can yield without confusion.

This is not beyond the reach of the local church. It is not reserved for a former generation. It is not limited to special meetings or unusual seasons. It belongs to the life of a Spirit-filled church that is willing to follow the Word.

A CHURCH THAT WELCOMES THE SPIRIT

A Holy Ghost church is not a church that tries to be sensational. It is not a church that chases manifestations for their own sake. It is not careless, loud, strange, or disorderly.

A Holy Ghost church honors the Word, welcomes the Spirit, and makes room for what God desires to do.

It teaches the people.

It cultivates expectation without pressure.

It allows time to wait upon the Lord.

It understands the difference between praying in tongues and giving a public message in tongues.

It welcomes interpretation.

It judges spiritual utterance by the Word.

It keeps peace in the house of God.

This is not complicated, but it does require intention. A church will rarely drift into this by accident. It must be taught, led, and shepherded.

READY FOR THE NEXT STEP

Now we are ready to take the next step.

We have seen that tongues are biblical. We have seen that tongues strengthen the believer. We have seen that tongues have a place in prayer and intercession. We have seen that tongues with interpretation belong in the gathered church. We have seen that Paul did not forbid tongues, but gave order so they could operate in peace.

In the next part of this book, we will move from what Scripture teaches to how we apply it. We will talk about making room in the service, expectation without pressure, preparing the congregation, leadership, and practical wisdom.

This is where many churches get stuck, but it does not have to remain that way.

The Word has not changed.

The Spirit has not left.

The gifts have not been withdrawn.

The command still stands.

"Forbid not to speak with tongues."

— 1 Corinthians 14:39

A Holy Ghost church hears that command, believes it, and makes room for the Spirit of God to move in the way Scripture reveals.

PART IV
A NEW PARADIGM

"How is it then, brethren? when ye come together, every one of you hath a psalm, hath a doctrine, hath a tongue, hath a revelation, hath an interpretation. Let all things be done unto edifying."
— 1 Corinthians 14:26

CHAPTER 22

THE ELEMENTS OF A CHURCH SERVICE

A paradigm is a way of seeing or understanding something. It is the pattern through which we think. When I speak of a new paradigm, I am not speaking of a new doctrine, a new revelation, or a new movement outside the Word of God. I am speaking of recovering the New Testament pattern for the gathered church. In 1 Corinthians 14:26, Paul shows a church where the Word is present, the Spirit is moving, the body is participating, and all things are done unto edifying.

When we speak of becoming a Holy Ghost church, the question will eventually arise: What should a service actually look like?

Many churches love the idea of the Spirit moving, but they are unsure how that fits into a real gathering. Some fear that allowing room for the Spirit will lead to confusion. Others assume it must require a complete restructuring of everything they already do.

But the New Testament does not leave us without a pattern.

Paul gives us a simple and clear picture of what can take place when the church comes together:

"How is it then, brethren? when ye come together, every one of you hath a psalm, hath a doctrine, hath a tongue, hath a revelation, hath an interpretation. Let all things be done unto edifying."

— 1 Corinthians 14:26

This one verse gives us a framework for a Holy Ghost church service. It is not complicated, but it is different from what many have experienced.

A SERVICE IS NOT BUILT AROUND ONE VOICE

One of the first things we notice is that the New Testament church was not centered around a single voice.

Paul did not say, "When you come together, the pastor has everything." He said, "every one of you hath."

This does not remove leadership. It places leadership in its proper role. Leadership teaches. Leadership guards. Leadership sets the tone. Leadership helps the body function in order.

But the body participates.

A Holy Ghost church is not built on spectators. It is built on believers who are taught, yielded, and ready to respond to God.

This does not mean everyone speaks in every service. It does not mean the service becomes open to anyone at any time. It means the congregation understands that the Holy Ghost may use members of the body for the edifying of the whole.

When believers understand that God can use them, something begins to change. They come to church not only to receive, but ready to respond.

THE CORE ELEMENTS

Paul lists several elements that may be present in a gathering:

- A psalm
- A doctrine
- A tongue
- A revelation
- An interpretation

These are not random. They show us the balance of a healthy church.

A psalm speaks of worship: hearts turned toward God.

A doctrine speaks of teaching: truth established in the Word.

A tongue and interpretation speak of supernatural utterance: the Spirit ministering to the congregation in a way that can be understood.

A revelation speaks of light: understanding, direction, or insight given by the Spirit.

This is not disorder. This is a complete service.

Many churches are strong in one or two of these areas. They may have excellent music and strong preaching, yet little room for revelation, tongues, or interpretation. Others may desire spiritual activity but lack the steadying influence of doctrine. A Holy Ghost church needs both.

The Word gives foundation.

Worship lifts the heart.

The Spirit gives utterance and understanding.

The body is edified.

That is the balance Paul describes.

THE GOAL: EDIFYING

Paul gives one simple boundary:

"Let all things be done unto edifying."

Everything that happens in a service should strengthen the people. The goal is not display. The goal is not emotionalism. The goal is not for something unusual to happen merely so people can say the service was spiritual.

The goal is edification.

If something strengthens the church, it may have a place. If it confuses, distracts, or draws attention away from Christ, it needs to be corrected or withheld.

This protects the move of the Spirit without shutting it down.

Edification keeps worship from becoming performance.

Edification keeps teaching from becoming lifeless information.

Edification keeps spiritual utterance from becoming display.

Edification keeps the whole service aimed at helping the body.

ORDER WITHOUT CONTROL

God is not the author of confusion. But neither is He the author of lifeless routine.

Order is not control. Order is clarity. It allows what God is doing to be understood and received.

A church can have structure and still leave room for the Spirit. In fact, structure often makes that room possible. A service can have worship, teaching, prayer, giving, ministry, and still include time to wait upon the Lord.

The issue is not whether a church has an order of service.

The issue is whether that order has any room for the Holy Ghost to move.

Structure should serve the Spirit's work, not crowd it out.

MAKING ROOM WITHOUT FORCING

A Holy Ghost church does not force spiritual activity. It makes space for the Spirit to move.

This may be as simple as allowing moments of waiting, teaching the congregation what to expect, recognizing when the Spirit is prompting, and not rushing past sacred moments.

A pastor may pause after worship and say:

"Let us wait before the Lord for a moment. We are not trying to force anything. We simply want to give room for the Holy Ghost to minister as He wills."

That moment does not have to be long. It does not have to be dramatic. It simply teaches the congregation that the service is not so hurried that the Spirit has no room.

The Spirit of God is not an interruption to a service. He is the reason for it.

A NEW EXPECTATION

Expectation changes everything.

A church that expects only empty routine will rarely rise above it. But when believers gather with the understanding that God may speak and move, hearts become attentive.

Faith rises.

People listen differently.

They respond differently.

They come ready.

Over time, what once felt unfamiliar becomes normal.

This does not mean every service will look the same. It does not mean tongues and interpretation will occur every time the church gathers. The Spirit divides as He wills. But it does mean the congregation is no longer surprised by the possibility of His moving.

They are taught.

They are peaceful.

They are ready.

RETURNING TO THE PATTERN

We are not inventing something new. We are returning to something original.

The New Testament church was not confused about what a gathering could include. They were taught. They understood. They participated.

A Holy Ghost church today can do the same.

Not by striving.

Not by forcing.

Not by imitating another church.

But by following Scripture.

A church service can be filled with worship, grounded in doctrine, open to revelation, and ready for tongues and interpretation. It can be orderly without being rigid. It can be spiritual without being confusing. It can be led well and still make room for the body to respond.

This is the kind of service Paul described.

And this is the kind of service a Holy Ghost church should be willing to recover.

CHAPTER 23

A NORMAL PART OF THE SERVICE

If we are going to make our churches Holy Ghost churches, then we must not only believe in the operation of the Spirit in theory. We must make room for His operation in practice.

One of the clearest places this applies is in the matter of a public tongue and interpretation in the church service.

Paul writes:

"How is it then, brethren? when ye come together, every one of you hath a psalm, hath a doctrine, hath a tongue, hath a revelation, hath an interpretation. Let all things be done unto edifying."

— 1 Corinthians 14:26

This verse does not present a tongue and an interpretation as strange intrusions into church life. Paul lists them as elements that may be present when believers gather. Alongside a psalm and a doctrine, he includes a tongue, a revelation, and an interpretation.

This does not mean a tongue and interpretation must be forced into every service any more than a sermon must be forced when the Spirit is leading the church to worship and wait before Him. There may be exceptions in any gathering. But exceptions should not become neglect. In the ordinary life of a Spirit-filled church, tongues and interpretation should be expected, welcomed, and given room, just as worship and the preaching of the Word are expected and given room.

That means a New Testament church should not treat this aspect of the service as unusual, risky, or reserved only for special occasions. Just as worship is expected, and just as preaching and teaching are expected, room should also be made for a public tongue and interpretation in the regular life of the church.

This is where many churches have missed it. They may say they believe in tongues. They may even say they believe in interpretation. But if no room is made, no expectation is taught, no preparation is made, and no instruction is given, then over time these things can slip into disuse.

Eventually the church arrives at a place where singing remains, doctrine remains, and preaching remains, but a tongue and interpretation are almost never heard. Once that happens, the people may begin to think such things were never meant to be normal at all.

But Paul did not write as if these things were accidental. He wrote as if they belonged in the gathering.

EXPECTED, NOT FORCED

This does not mean tongues and interpretation are to be forced. The Holy Ghost is not honored by imitation or pressure. A public tongue should not be manufactured any more than prophecy should be manufactured.

Yet there is a great difference between forcing something and making room for it.

Churches prepare for worship. Churches prepare for preaching. Churches set aside time for singing, teaching, prayer, and ministry. In the same way, leadership can prepare the church to expect that a tongue, a revelation, and an interpretation may be part of what takes place when believers gather.

That expectation matters.

When a church never expects a public tongue, the people do not yield to it. When leadership never teaches on it, believers grow unfamiliar with it. When no time is given for it, those who may sense the Spirit prompting them learn to suppress that prompting and remain silent.

Then the church wonders why these manifestations have become rare.

The answer is simple: what is ignored becomes uncommon. What is taught, welcomed, and expected becomes normal.

A Holy Ghost church should therefore not merely tolerate the possibility of a public tongue. It should recognize it as a legitimate and expected element of a New Testament gathering.

Consistent practice also helps the church become more proficient in the operation of the gifts. This does not mean the gifts are man-made or produced by human effort. The utterance is still given by the Spirit. But when believers are taught and given regular opportunity to yield, they learn to respond with greater peace, sensitivity, and confidence. Those who give a public tongue become more comfortable stepping out in faith. Those who interpret, including pastors and leaders, grow in sensitivity when there is regular opportunity for the gift to operate.

The church learns to move with the Spirit in a steady, reverent flow.

TONGUES IN PRAYER AND WORSHIP

This is not the only way tongues may be expressed in a service. Believers may pray in the Spirit together. They may worship in tongues. They may sing in the Spirit.

Paul says:

"For he that speaketh in an unknown tongue speaketh not unto men, but unto God..."

— 1 Corinthians 14:2

And again:

"For if I pray in an unknown tongue, my spirit prayeth..."

— 1 Corinthians 14:14

And again:

"I will pray with the spirit... I will sing with the spirit..."

— 1 Corinthians 14:15

Romans also tells us:

"Likewise the Spirit also helpeth our infirmities..."

— Romans 8:26

So yes, there is a place in the service for prayer in the Spirit, worship in the Spirit, singing in the Spirit, and intercession in the Spirit. Those expressions are directed toward God and are part of the spiritual life of the congregation.

A church may have a season in a service where believers pray in the Spirit together. There may be moments after singing when the people remain before the Lord, worshiping in other tongues. All of that is scriptural and belongs in the life of a Spirit-filled church.

But alongside those Godward expressions, Paul also identifies something more specific: a tongue, a revelation, and an interpretation.

This is not merely the congregation praying unto God. It is

part of the public ministry of the service, one of the ways God may address His people in the assembly.

That is why it must not be neglected.

GIVING IT A PLACE

A church should prepare for this. Leadership should teach the people that tongues and interpretation are part of the normal life of a Spirit-filled church. Time should be made for waiting upon the Lord. Space should be given so that individuals who sense the Spirit's leading may yield to a public tongue.

The church should understand that this is no stranger than a psalm or a doctrine. It is one of the elements of the gathering.

Again, this does not mean every person must speak publicly. It does not mean a tongue must be produced on command. It does not mean the service becomes awkward or artificial.

It means leadership expects the Holy Ghost to move in this way and therefore gives Him room to do so.

A pastor may simply pause after worship and say:

"Let us wait before the Lord for a moment. If the Spirit gives a public tongue, we will wait for the interpretation so the church may be edified."

That is not pressure. That is room.

A church that never makes room for a public tongue will rarely hear one. A church that never expects interpretation will eventually lose sensitivity to it. But a church that teaches these things, honors them, and gives them place in the service will begin to see them operate with greater regularity and confidence.

PRESERVING PROPER USE

This is one reason Paul's instruction is so important. He is not merely correcting abuse. He is preserving proper use.

He is showing the church how these things can remain active without falling into confusion.

He also tells us the purpose of such ministry:

"Now, brethren, if I come unto you speaking with tongues, what shall I profit you, except I shall speak to you either by revelation, or by knowledge, or by prophesying, or by doctrine?"

— 1 Corinthians 14:6

That verse gives us the value of interpretation. When a tongue is interpreted, profit comes to the church by revelation, knowledge, prophesying, or doctrine.

This is not empty speech. It is not emotional display. It is divine utterance brought into understandable form so the church may be helped.

As with prophecy, what is spoken should remain in harmony with the revealed Word of God and the character of God. It should edify, exhort, and comfort. It should strengthen the people, not confuse them.

A public tongue and interpretation are not lesser matters. They are part of how God ministers to His people in the assembly.

THE FULLER PICTURE

In many churches, singing is expected. Preaching is expected. Announcements are expected. But a tongue and interpretation are treated as though they belonged to some other age or some unusual kind of meeting.

That is not Paul's picture of church life.

He said:

"How is it then, brethren? when ye come together, every one of you hath a psalm, hath a doctrine, hath a tongue, hath a revelation, hath an interpretation. Let all things be done unto edifying."

— 1 Corinthians 14:26

Paul's picture is fuller than what many churches have known. He includes worship. He includes doctrine. He includes revelation. He includes a tongue. He includes an interpretation. All of it is to serve one purpose: edification.

A Holy Ghost church should therefore teach this, expect this, prepare for this, and make room for this.

Not by forcing it.

Not by imitating someone else.

Not by making the service awkward.

But by honoring the Scriptures and allowing the Spirit liberty to move.

If we do not, we may slowly drift back into the same condition that has left many churches with doctrine but little manifestation, structure but little spiritual utterance, and sound teaching but little present expression of the Spirit among the people.

If we are going to be a Holy Ghost church, then a public tongue and interpretation must not be left to chance. They must be understood as a normal and expected part of the gathered life of the church.

CHAPTER 24

ONE INTERPRETER

If a public tongue is to have a normal place in the church service, then it must also be governed by scriptural order.

The Holy Ghost does not produce confusion. He does not inspire competition. He does not lead people to interrupt one another, talk over one another, or try to improve upon one another's interpretation. When the gifts of the Spirit operate in purity, they also operate in clarity, peace, and order.

This truth did not begin in the New Testament. Even in the Old Testament, when God's presence was manifested among His people, there was a right way to approach it, a right way to handle it, and a right order connected to it.

THE ARK AND THE VOICE OF GOD

Under the Old Covenant, the ark of the covenant represented the presence of God in a unique and sacred way. It was connected with the voice of God and the manifestation of His presence among His people.

The Lord said to Moses:

"And there I will meet with thee, and I will commune with thee from above the mercy seat, from between the two cherubims which are upon the ark of the testimony..."

— Exodus 25:22

And again the Bible says:

"And when Moses was gone into the tabernacle of the congregation to speak with him, then he heard the voice of one speaking unto him from off the mercy seat that was upon the ark of testimony, from between the two cherubims..."

— Numbers 7:89

The ark was not merely a religious object. It was associated with God meeting His people and speaking among them.

This gives us an important type and shadow. When we talk about God speaking in the church through a public tongue and interpretation, we are dealing with something sacred. We are not dealing with mere emotional display or human expression. We are dealing with divine utterance among the people of God.

DUE ORDER

In 1 Chronicles 13, David desired to bring the ark back. His desire was right. His hunger was right. His intention was right. But something went wrong.

The ark was placed on a new cart, and when Uzzah reached out his hand to steady it, judgment followed. The Bible says:

"And David was displeased, because the LORD had made a breach upon Uzza..."

— 1 Chronicles 13:11

And then:

"And David was afraid of God that day, saying, How shall I bring the ark of God home to me?"

— 1 Chronicles 13:12

David did not lose his desire for the presence of God. But he became afraid because the presence had not been handled properly.

Many churches have responded similarly to the move of the Spirit. They have seen confusion, flesh, disorder, or public manifestations handled poorly. Because of that, they became afraid of the whole subject. Instead of returning to Scripture and learning how to handle the presence of God rightly, they set the matter aside.

But that was not David's final response, and it should not be ours.

When David later revisited the matter, he returned to the Word of God and discovered that the ark had to be handled according to divine order.

"Then David said, None ought to carry the ark of God but the Levites..."

— 1 Chronicles 15:2

And again:

"For because ye did it not at the first, the LORD our God made a breach upon us, for that we sought him not after the due order."

— 1 Chronicles 15:13

That phrase is vital: "after the due order."

David's problem was not that he desired the presence of God. His problem was that he had not sought God after the due order.

That is exactly the issue many churches face with the gifts of the Spirit. The answer is not to remove them. The answer is not to fear them. The answer is not to silence them. The answer is to seek God after the due order.

That is what Paul is doing in 1 Corinthians 14. He is not abolishing spiritual utterance in the church. He is showing the church the due order by which it is to function.

When Paul says:

"Let all things be done decently and in order."

— 1 Corinthians 14:40

he is not quenching the Spirit. He is protecting the move of the Spirit by restoring due order to it.

ONE INTERPRETER

With that background in mind, Paul gives this instruction:

"If any man speak in an unknown tongue, let it be by two, or at the most by three, and that by course; and let one interpret."

— 1 Corinthians 14:27

That instruction is simple, but it is weighty.

In a given service, Paul allows for two, or at the most three, different persons to speak publicly in tongues. Then he says, "let one interpret." This means that while more than one person may give a public tongue, one recognized interpreter should bring the interpretations for the public utterances given in that service. That preserves order and keeps the congregation from confusion.

This does not mean only one person in the whole church is capable of interpretation. Neither does it mean that God could never use another person in another service or on another occasion. It means that in a given service, for the sake of order, one interpreter should be recognized to interpret the public tongues that are given.

That is wisdom.

There may be several people in a congregation who have the spiritual capability to interpret. But if all of them assume they should respond in the same service, the result may be confusion rather than clarity. One may begin, another may feel dissatisfied and attempt to give a second interpretation, and yet another may try to improve upon what was already given. That is not excellence. That is disorder.

When that happens, the congregation is no longer focused on what God is saying. It becomes aware of uncertainty, rivalry, or confusion. The purity of the manifestation is clouded, and the beauty of the gift is diminished.

This is one reason Paul says, "let one interpret."

A recognized interpreter helps protect the service from confusion. A recognized interpreter helps preserve unity. A recognized interpreter provides consistency so the church can receive what is being spoken without distraction.

WHY THE PASTOR IS OFTEN THE CLEAREST CHOICE

Very often, the pastor may be the most natural interpreter in a church service.

This is not because no one else could ever interpret. It is not because the pastor must always interpret. But in many churches, the pastor will often be the clearest candidate for several reasons.

First, more often than not, he is the one person most grounded in the Scriptures. Since interpretation must line up with the Word of God and carry genuine spiritual substance, scriptural grounding matters greatly.

Second, he is usually the one directing the service. He understands the flow of the meeting, the tone of the service, and the spiritual direction in which things are moving. Because of that, he is often in a good position to recognize how a public tongue fits within what the Spirit is doing in that moment.

Third, he is usually the most recognized voice in the service. The people know him. They trust him. They are less likely to dismiss his words casually. That matters, because interpretation is given for the edification of the church. If the church does not receive the interpretation, its value is lost.

Of course, these same qualifications may exist in another individual. There may be someone in the church who is spiritually mature, scripturally grounded, experienced, respected, and clearly gifted to interpret. There may also be times when the pastor himself does not feel that interpretation is his strongest area of gifting. In such cases, another qualified person may be the proper interpreter.

But in general, the pastor often makes the most sense.

SUPERNATURAL GIFTS THROUGH PREPARED VESSELS

This also reminds us of something important: even though these are supernatural gifts, they still flow through prepared vessels.

The Spirit of God is the source.

The ability is divine.

The utterance is supernatural.

But the vessel matters.

A person's scriptural understanding, spiritual development, experience, and background knowledge may greatly affect his ability to interpret clearly. One individual may be far more equipped than another, not because God loves him more, but because he has become a more prepared vessel.

That should not trouble us. It should instruct us.

We do not deny the supernatural nature of the gifts. But neither do we pretend that preparation does not matter. God uses yielded vessels, but He also uses prepared vessels. And when the vessel is both yielded and prepared, the quality of the interpretation may be clearer and more profitable to the church.

This is another reason a recognized interpreter is so important.

WHAT THE INTERPRETATION MUST BE

The interpretation does not create the message; it gives the meaning of the message already spoken in the tongue. The public tongue is the original utterance. The interpretation brings that utterance into the understanding of the congregation. For that reason, both the tongue and the interpretation must be treated with reverence.

The interpreter should not be chosen carelessly. Interpretation is not a casual assignment. It is not simply a matter of willingness. It requires spiritual preparation, scriptural knowledge, maturity, sensitivity to the Holy Ghost, and an understanding of the purpose of the gift.

Paul says:

"Now, brethren, if I come unto you speaking with tongues, what shall I profit you, except I shall speak to you either by revelation, or by knowledge, or by prophesying, or by doctrine?"

— 1 Corinthians 14:6

That means the interpretation must carry real substance. It should bring revelation, or knowledge, or prophesying, or doctrine. It should not be vague, careless, or disconnected from biblical truth.

Interpretation must also remain in harmony with Scripture and the character of God. God will not inspire a message that contradicts His written Word. He will not speak contrary to His nature. And because interpretation functions much like simple prophecy in its effect, it should carry the same general quality Paul gives for prophecy:

"But he that prophesieth speaketh unto men to edification, and exhortation, and comfort."

— 1 Corinthians 14:3

This does not mean every interpretation will sound soft or gentle in tone. But it does mean it should build up the church, strengthen the people, and remain spiritually sound. It should not produce fear, confusion, embarrassment, or condemnation as its primary fruit.

That is why the interpreter must be qualified.

Qualified does not mean famous.

Qualified does not mean dramatic.

Qualified does not mean merely willing.

It means spiritually prepared, scripturally grounded, experienced, and mature enough to handle the gift with reverence.

NO COMPETING INTERPRETATIONS

In many churches, lack of order has damaged confidence in the gifts. Some have allowed multiple interpretations of the same tongue simply because different people were dissatisfied with the first. One person gives an interpretation, and another rises to reinterpret it. That only displays disorder and confusion.

It suggests that the church is not listening carefully.

It suggests that people are competing rather than cooperating.

It suggests that the gifts are being handled casually.

This should not be so.

The gifts of the Spirit can operate in purity and order.

They can operate with clarity.

They can operate with excellence.

They can provide a good example of order in the church service.

This is not accomplished by silencing the gifts. It is accomplished by stewarding them properly.

In practical terms, leadership should know who among the people are spiritually mature and prepared to interpret. There may be several such individuals in the life of a church, but that does not mean all of them should function in the same service. One interpreter should be recognized for that service so that tongues given by two or three individuals may be interpreted clearly and in order.

That brings peace to the congregation.

It protects the service from confusion.

It allows the people to focus on the message rather than the mechanics.

And it upholds the dignity and purity of the gift.

IF THERE IS NO INTERPRETER

Paul also gives the necessary safeguard:

"But if there be no interpreter, let him keep silence in the church; and let him speak to himself, and to God."

— 1 Corinthians 14:28

This is not a denial of tongues. It is a protection of order. If no interpreter is present, then the one who senses a public tongue should not deliver it to the church. He may still speak to himself and to God, but the public expression is withheld because the interpretation required for edification is not available.

This shows again how seriously Paul treats the matter. The public tongue is not forbidden. It is regulated so that the church may be helped.

A Holy Ghost church should therefore do more than desire manifestations. It should establish scriptural order for those manifestations. It should make room for a public tongue. It should expect interpretation. And it should recognize that one prepared, qualified, recognized interpreter in a service is not a restriction of the Spirit, but a protection of His work.

When this is understood, the church no longer fears the gifts. It learns how to receive them.

The people begin to see that spiritual utterance need not be chaotic. They begin to hear the voice of God in ways that strengthen faith. And the standard of excellence in the service rises, because the gifts are no longer left to confusion, but are handled with the purity, clarity, and due order that Scripture requires.

CHAPTER 25

MANY MEMBERS, ONE BODY

If a church is going to become a Holy Ghost church, it must understand not only that the Spirit gives utterance, but also that He distributes His workings among many members in one body.

A healthy church does not depend on only one expression, one voice, or one vessel. It is a body, and a body has many members. Yet the fact that there are many members does not mean there is confusion. Diversity is not disorder. Variety is not chaos. In the church, God joins multiplicity with harmony.

Paul teaches this throughout 1 Corinthians. There are diversities of gifts, differences of administrations, and diversities of operations, but it is the same Lord, the same Spirit, and the same God who worketh all in all. The body is not one member, but many. That means we should expect different members to function in different ways.

One may give a tongue.
Another may interpret.
Another may prophesy.

Another may judge.

Another may lead the flow of the service.

Another may simply learn and receive.

Yet all of this belongs to one body.

This truth helps us avoid two opposite errors.

The first error is to think that because the Spirit moves, everyone should speak whenever he pleases. That is not the teaching of Scripture.

The second error is to think that because not everyone functions publicly, only one person matters. That is not the teaching of Scripture either.

The church is one body with many members, and each member has his place.

ORDERED MINISTRY IN THE ASSEMBLY

Paul says:

"Let the prophets speak two or three, and let the other judge."

— 1 Corinthians 14:29

This is important.

Paul is not describing a service where endless numbers of people all rise to speak publicly. He is describing ordered ministry in the church. Just as he gave order for tongues, he also gives order for prophecy.

"Two or three" sets a practical boundary. The point is not to encourage unlimited expression. The point is to allow genuine spiritual utterance while preserving peace and edification.

In that sense, these verses especially concern those who function as leaders, prophets, or recognized ministry vessels in the assembly. Paul is dealing with public ministry, not unchecked spontaneity from an entire crowd.

There is liberty, but there is also government. There is room, but there is also restraint.

SPEAKING FIRST, THEN JUDGING

Paul does not only say, "Let the prophets speak two or three." He also says, "and let the other judge."

That order matters.

The utterance is given, and then it is judged.

This is a needed correction in many churches. Sometimes there is no utterance at all because everything is judged prematurely. People become so cautious, hesitant, and fearful of getting it wrong that nothing is ever spoken.

But Paul's instruction does not create silence before the utterance. It creates discernment after the utterance.

The church must hear what is spoken, and then those who are mature and qualified must judge it properly. That is a much healthier pattern.

If everything is suppressed before it is spoken, the church may appear safe, but it is no longer functioning the way Paul described. A Holy Ghost church must learn how to allow utterance and then apply judgment, rather than shutting down utterance altogether.

This does not mean careless speech is encouraged. It means the proper place of judgment is maintained. The church hears, weighs, and discerns what has been said.

YIELDED, BUT STILL RESPONSIBLE

Paul continues:

"If any thing be revealed to another that sitteth by, let the first hold his peace.

For ye may all prophesy one by one, that all may learn, and all may be comforted.

And the spirits of the prophets are subject to the prophets."

— 1 Corinthians 14:30–32

These verses are full of wisdom.

First, they show that spiritual utterance can function in an orderly way. If something is revealed to another, the first can hold his peace. That means spiritual people are not out of control. They are not seized by some irresistible force that makes them unable to wait, stop, or defer to the order of the service.

This is true not only for prophecy, but by principle for tongues and interpretation as well. A person may feel the anointing strongly and still remain capable of waiting for the right moment. A person may sense the Spirit prompting and still yield to the order of the house. A person may be ready to speak and yet hold his peace until the proper time.

That is not quenching the Spirit. That is cooperating with Him in peace.

This truth is extremely important because some have acted as though a person under the influence of the Spirit loses all control. Paul teaches the opposite. "The spirits of the prophets are subject to the prophets." In other words, the person remains responsible for how and when he yields.

God does not remove self-control in order to produce spiritual ministry.

That principle protects the church from confusion.

NOT EVERYONE AT ONCE

When Paul says, "ye may all prophesy one by one," he is not picturing a service where hundreds of people all give public prophecy one after another. He has already given the boundaries. He has already said, "Let the prophets speak two or three."

So the "all" must be understood within the framework of orderly, recognized ministry in the assembly, not as unlimited public participation by the whole congregation.

That is important to say plainly.

Otherwise, people read the verse without the surrounding order and imagine a service with no practical boundaries at all. But Paul is doing the opposite. He is showing that those who are permitted to function publicly can do so one by one, in a way that allows all to learn and all to be comforted.

The purpose, again, is edification.

People learn.

People are comforted.

People are helped.

That can only happen where peace is preserved.

GOD IS NOT THE AUTHOR OF CONFUSION

Paul then says:

"For God is not the author of confusion, but of peace, as in all churches of the saints."

— 1 Corinthians 14:33

That statement governs the whole chapter.

God is not the source of confusion. If a service is marked by interruption, rivalry, uncertainty, and disorder, that is not something to excuse by saying, "The Spirit was moving." The Spirit of God moves in peace. His manifestations may be powerful, but they are not chaotic. His utterances may be supernatural, but they are not disorderly.

Peace is not the absence of spiritual activity.

Peace is the atmosphere in which spiritual activity can be rightly received.

That is why the body must understand its function. Many members do not mean many directions. Many members do not mean many competing voices. Many members do not mean a lack of government. They mean that the same Spirit may use different people at different times, all within the peace and order of the local church.

THE PLACE OF LEADERS

This is where leadership matters again.

Leaders help maintain the peace of the service. Leaders recognize who is ready to function. Leaders judge what is spoken. Leaders know when to wait, when to proceed, and when correction is needed.

Leadership does not replace the Holy Ghost, but it does help steward the flow of the Holy Ghost in the assembly.

That is one reason these verses should not be read in a loose and careless way. Paul is not giving permission for spiritual confusion. He is showing how mature ministry functions in the church.

Where there is no leadership, people may all feel equally free to speak.

Where there is no judgment, people may assume every utterance is automatically correct.

Where there is no order, confusion grows quickly.

But where leaders understand Scripture and help guide the service, the people gain confidence. They see that the gifts of the Spirit can function in beauty, purity, and peace.

EVERY MEMBER MATTERS

Even with all this emphasis on order, we must not lose the main point: the church is still a body with many members.

Not everyone will give a tongue, interpret, prophesy publicly, or lead. But every member matters. The one who speaks, the one who interprets, the one who judges, and the one who receives instruction and comfort all have a place in the body's life together.

A Holy Ghost church is not built by expecting one person to carry the whole ministry while everyone else remains passive. Nor is it built by letting everyone do whatever they please. It is built when each member understands his place, honors the place of others, and functions under the peace and order of the Spirit.

PEACE GOVERNS THE GATHERING

The goal of all this is not simply activity. The goal is a church where the Spirit is welcomed, the members are functioning, and peace governs the whole gathering.

When that happens, spiritual utterance is no longer feared.

It is no longer chaotic.

It is no longer treated as strange.

It becomes part of the healthy life of the body.

Then the church begins to look more like the New Testament pattern:

many members,
many functions,
many vessels,
but one body,
one Spirit,

and one atmosphere of peace.

That is the kind of church Paul envisioned. And that is the kind of church we should desire to become.

PART V
CONSIDER YOUR WAYS

"Thus saith the LORD of hosts; Consider your ways.
Go up to the mountain, and bring wood, and build the house;
and I will take pleasure in it, and I will be glorified, saith the
LORD."
— Haggai 1:7–8

CHAPTER 26

THINGS TO CONSIDER IN A HOLY GHOST CHURCH

When Haggai told God's people to **"consider your ways"** in **Haggai 1:7–8**, he was speaking concerning the rebuilding of the house of the Lord. The people had become occupied with their own houses while the Lord's house lay waste. Yet the principle still speaks to us. We must consider our ways and ask whether we are building according to God's pleasure, God's glory, and God's order. A Holy Ghost church is not built by accident. It is built when God's people give attention to what He has commanded and make room for what He desires.

By this point, the question is no longer whether the New Testament church should welcome the moving of the Holy Ghost. Scripture has already answered that.

The question now is one of stewardship.

How should a church that desires the moving of the Spirit conduct itself? What attitudes should be present? What mistakes should be avoided? What practical considerations help preserve both liberty and order?

These are important questions because it is possible to be

right in doctrine, yet careless in practice. It is possible to believe in the gifts of the Spirit and still mishandle them. It is possible to desire the presence of God and yet fail to seek Him after the due order.

That is why this final section matters.

We are not turning away from spiritual things by becoming practical. We are protecting spiritual things by becoming practical. The Holy Ghost does not dishonor wisdom. He works beautifully where there is humility, reverence, maturity, and scriptural understanding.

A church that wants to be a Holy Ghost church must therefore be willing to consider its ways.

A CHURCH MUST BE HONEST ABOUT ITS CONDITION

One of the first things a church must do is deal honestly with where it really is.

Some churches say they believe in the Holy Ghost, but in practice there is no room for Him to move. There may be good preaching, good music, and good people, but no expectation of spiritual utterance, no waiting upon God, and little awareness that He may wish to speak in a present and living way.

Other churches may allow some expression, but without enough teaching, order, or pastoral oversight to preserve purity.

Still others may have known seasons of genuine manifestation in the past, but have slowly drifted into disuse because what was once valued is no longer expected.

A church will not be helped by pretending.

If the gifts have been ignored, that should be admitted.

If fear has silenced the people, that should be admitted.

If excess has created confusion, that should be admitted.

If spiritual things have been treated casually, that should be admitted.

Truth is never helped by pretending that everything is fine when it is not.

DESIRE IS NOT ENOUGH

A church may sincerely desire a move of the Spirit, but desire by itself is not enough.

David desired the ark of God, but desire alone did not keep him from error. The ark had to be handled after the due order. In the same way, a church may desire spiritual manifestations, but if it does not teach the people, prepare the people, and establish biblical order, desire alone will not be enough.

What is needed is not only hunger, but understanding.

Not only zeal, but wisdom.

Not only liberty, but government.

The answer is never to remove the Spirit from church life. The answer is to make room for the Spirit according to Scripture.

CHURCHES BECOME WHAT THEY CONSISTENTLY PRACTICE

This is one of the great practical truths of ministry: a church usually becomes what it consistently practices.

If a church consistently makes room only for music and preaching, then music and preaching will become the full extent of its expectation.

If a church consistently teaches the people to wait upon the Lord, recognize the Spirit's prompting, honor a public tongue, and receive interpretation, then over time those things become part of the church's normal life.

What is practiced becomes familiar.

What is familiar becomes expected.

What is expected becomes part of the culture of the house.

That is why churches must consider their ways carefully. A church rarely drifts into Holy Ghost order by accident.

It must be taught, led, and cultivated.

MATURITY MATTERS

Not every problem in a church service is a doctrinal problem. Some problems are maturity problems.

People may genuinely love God and still need to grow in timing. They may be sincere and still need to grow in wisdom. They may have a real experience with the Spirit and still need help understanding how to function in a gathered assembly.

That should not discourage us. It should remind us that growth is part of church life.

A Holy Ghost church is not a church where everyone is already perfect. It is a church where the people are learning how to walk in love, yield to the Spirit, honor leadership, and function in peace.

This is one reason teaching matters so much. People often do better when they understand better.

LOVE MUST REMAIN CENTRAL

No matter how strongly we emphasize the gifts of the Spirit, we must never lose sight of the greater context Paul gives in 1 Corinthians.

The gifts matter.

Order matters.

Interpretation matters.

Public utterance matters.

But love still governs everything.

A church can become so eager for manifestations that it neglects the spirit in which those manifestations are to operate. That is always dangerous. Love protects the church from harshness, competition, pride, and spiritual vanity.

If people are trying to be heard more than they are trying to help, something is already wrong. If people are eager to correct one another publicly, outshine one another, or prove they are more spiritual, the atmosphere is already moving away from the Spirit of Christ.

The Holy Ghost and the love of God do not work against one another. They work together.

THE GOAL IS NOT ACTIVITY, BUT EDIFICATION

A church should never pursue manifestations simply to say that manifestations are present.

The goal is not activity for activity's sake.

The goal is not a dramatic atmosphere.

The goal is not spiritual display.

The goal is edification.

Everything that happens in the service should strengthen the body, honor Christ, and agree with the Word of God. If a practice consistently produces confusion, distraction, or fleshly attention, it needs correction. If it strengthens the people and magnifies Christ, it should be valued.

This helps keep the church balanced. We do not reject the gifts because they can be abused. Neither do we excuse disorder simply because something spiritual is claimed. We weigh things by their agreement with Scripture and their fruit in the body.

WE ARE STEWARDING REVELATION

We are not dealing merely with order for order's sake. We are dealing with the stewardship of revelation.

When Paul described the gathered church as having a psalm, a doctrine, a tongue, a revelation, and an interpretation, he showed us that spiritual utterance in the assembly was not meant to end in mystery alone, but in understanding and profit.

A public tongue is not meaningless sound. It is the original utterance given by the Spirit. The interpretation does not create a different message; it brings the meaning of that utterance into language the congregation can understand. In that sense, the tongue itself should never be belittled. It is a true manifestation of the Spirit, and the interpretation allows the church to receive its benefit.

This is no small matter.

When tongues and interpretation operate rightly, the church is not merely having an experience. The church is receiving understanding, direction, and help by the Spirit of God.

This also helps us understand why interpretation must be handled carefully. If interpretation brings the meaning of a Spirit-given utterance to the church, then it must agree with the revealed Word of God, the character of God, and the testimony of Jesus Christ. The angel said to John, "the testimony of Jesus is the spirit of prophecy" (Revelation 19:10). That means true spiritual utterance will not pull the church away from Christ, but will bear witness to Him.

It is not enough for something to sound spiritual. It must be spiritually true, scripturally sound, and Christ-honoring.

That is why these practical considerations matter so much. We are not merely trying to avoid confusion. We are seeking to preserve a place where the voice of the Spirit may be heard clearly, peacefully, and in order.

PASTORS MUST BE COURAGEOUS AND CAREFUL

A great deal rests upon leadership.

Pastors must be courageous enough to teach what Scripture teaches, even when people are unfamiliar with it. They must be willing to make room for what God has placed in the church, even if it has been neglected for years.

At the same time, they must be careful enough to guard the service from confusion and excess.

This is not always easy. It requires prayer, patience, wisdom, and firmness. But it is part of pastoral stewardship. The pastor is not the Holy Ghost, but he is responsible for the atmosphere in which the people are taught to respond to the Holy Ghost.

A timid pastor may leave the church dry.

If these things are handled carelessly from the pulpit, the church may be left confused.

A wise pastor helps the church walk in both liberty and order.

THE CHURCH MUST LEARN TO RECEIVE

A Holy Ghost church is not shaped only by those who speak. It is also shaped by those who hear.

The people must learn how to receive spiritual utterance. They must learn reverence. They must learn discernment. They must learn that when God speaks, whether by preaching, prophecy, a public tongue with interpretation, or spiritual song, the right response is not casual indifference but spiritual attentiveness.

A church that does not know how to receive will not benefit fully even when the gifts are present.

This is one reason repeated teaching is necessary. The congregation must understand not only what is happening, but why it matters.

THIS FINAL SECTION

In the chapters ahead, we will look more closely at several practical considerations.

We will consider things to keep in mind when giving a tongue, things to keep in mind when interpreting a tongue, things to keep in mind when judging prophecy, and why a Holy Ghost church is both reasonable and necessary in our day.

These are not small matters. They are part of the due order that protects the moving of the Spirit in the local church.

If we will consider our ways honestly, submit ourselves to the Word of God, and remain yielded to the Holy Ghost, then our churches can move beyond dead formality without falling into confusion. We can become churches where the Word is honored, the Spirit is welcomed, and the voice of God is heard with clarity, peace, and power.

That is not beyond reach.

That is not reserved for another generation.

That is the pattern still given to the Church.

CHAPTER 27

THINGS TO CONSIDER WHEN GIVING A TONGUE

If a church is going to make room for a public tongue in the service, then believers must be taught how to handle that privilege reverently and wisely.

A public tongue is not a casual matter. It is not merely a moment of excitement, nor is it an opportunity for personal expression. If a person gives a tongue publicly in the church, he is stepping into a sacred moment in which God desires to edify His people through spiritual utterance and interpretation. That should never be treated lightly.

Paul writes:

"If any man speak in an unknown tongue, let it be by two, or at the most by three, and that by course; and let one interpret."

— 1 Corinthians 14:27

That verse alone tells us that a public tongue in the church is not to be careless, random, or without order. It is to be governed by Scripture so that the people may be edified and the peace of the service preserved.

With that in mind, there are several things a believer should consider before giving a public tongue.

BE SURE IT IS DIRECTED TO THE CHURCH

Not every expression in tongues belongs in the same category.

As we have already seen, there are times when believers may pray in the Spirit, worship in the Spirit, sing in the Spirit, or speak mysteries unto God. Those expressions are real, scriptural, and valuable. But a public tongue given in the church is different. It is not merely private prayer made louder. It is not simply a personal blessing expressed publicly. It is a spiritual utterance that must be interpreted for the edification of the church.

That means the first question a person should consider is this:

Is the Holy Ghost prompting me to give this publicly to the church, or is it something between God and me?

That distinction matters greatly.

Many things that are genuine spiritually are still meant to remain between the believer and the Lord. Paul said:

"But if there be no interpreter, let him keep silence in the church; and let him speak to himself, and to God."

— 1 Corinthians 14:28

Paul's instruction is plain: if there is no interpreter, the person should keep silence in the church.

ACT IN FAITH, NOT EMOTION ALONE

A public tongue is not given merely because a person feels stirred. It is given as an act of faith in response to the Spirit and in obedience to the Word of God.

Paul's language assumes that spiritual utterance has a place in the assembly. A psalm has a place. Doctrine has a place. A tongue has a place. Revelation has a place. Interpretation has a place. All of it must be governed by edification.

He also says, "forbid not to speak with tongues." Therefore, when a believer yields to give a public tongue in the proper order, he is not acting on impulse alone. He is acting in faith upon what the Word of God permits and teaches.

This is important.

Faith is not presumption. Faith does not ignore order. Faith does not push past leadership or disregard the peace of the service. But faith does respond when the Spirit prompts and the Word permits.

A person giving a public tongue should not think, "I am doing this because I am emotional." He should understand, "I am yielding to the Holy Ghost in faith, according to Scripture, so that the church may be edified through interpretation."

That keeps the act sacred.

The tongue itself may be a mystery to the understanding, but it is not meaningless. Paul said:

"For he that speaketh in an unknown tongue speaketh not unto men, but unto God: for no man understandeth him; howbeit in the spirit he speaketh mysteries."

— 1 Corinthians 14:2

When a tongue is given publicly and then interpreted, what was mystery becomes understandable to the congregation. Through interpretation, the church receives the benefit of what the Spirit has uttered.

So the believer who gives the tongue is acting in faith that the Spirit is giving utterance, and that God desires the congregation to be edified when the interpretation comes.

DO NOT SPEAK JUST BECAUSE YOU FEEL STIRRED

A person may feel deeply stirred in the Spirit and yet still need to wait for wisdom and timing.

Spiritual stirring alone is not enough to justify public speech. A believer may be blessed, moved, or built up inwardly and still not be called to give a public tongue. This is one reason maturity matters. The one who would speak publicly must learn the difference between personal edification and public utterance.

A public tongue should not come forth merely because the person feels emotional, excited, or strongly impressed. It should come because there is a genuine prompting of the Spirit to speak to the church in that moment, and because the person is acting in faith according to the Word.

That is why self-control remains important. The Spirit of God does not overpower people in a way that removes responsibility. What God gives must still be stewarded by the believer.

CONSIDER THE TIMING

Even when a tongue is genuine, timing still matters.

A person may sense the leading of the Spirit but need to wait for the right moment. He may feel the prompting during a transition in the service, while someone is already speaking, or while leadership is moving in another direction. In such moments, wisdom is needed.

Paul says:

"And the spirits of the prophets are subject to the prophets."

— 1 Corinthians 14:32

By principle, this applies here as well. A person under the anointing is not out of control. He can wait. He can hold his peace. He can yield at the right time. He can recognize that the Spirit of God is not the author of confusion.

A well-timed tongue can open the way for revelation and blessing in the service. A poorly timed one, even if sincere, may create distraction and confusion. So the one who would speak publicly must learn to sense not only the prompting, but also the proper moment.

RESPECT THE SCRIPTURAL LIMIT

A person who gives a public tongue must also respect the limit Paul gives.

Paul said:

"If any man speak in an unknown tongue, let it be by two, or at the most by three, and that by course; and let one interpret."

— 1 Corinthians 14:27

The words "at the most by three" matter. They show that public tongues in a service are not unlimited.

This appears to refer to the number of individuals speaking publicly, not simply the number of short utterances. One person may give a tongue and continue until the utterance is complete. But once he is settled, at peace, and the flow has moved on to another person or another part of the service, he should not keep returning to give more public tongues.

That requires humility.

A yielded person is not only willing to speak. He is also willing to stop. He is willing to let another function. He is willing to let the service move forward.

Once two or three individuals have functioned publicly in tongues and interpretation has been given, the church should honor Paul's boundary and move on with the rest of the service. There are other things that may need to be accomplished in the gathering, including preaching, teaching, prayer, ministry, worship, and pastoral direction.

This is not quenching the Spirit. It is obeying the order the Spirit gave through Scripture.

STAY IN PEACE

A public tongue should come from a place of peace, not pressure.

If a person feels driven, agitated, frantic, or panicked, that is not the best condition in which to speak publicly. The Holy Ghost moves in peace. His presence may be powerful, but it is not disorderly.

A believer should therefore learn to yield from a place of inward confidence and peace. He does not have to force his way into the service. He does not have to make something happen. He does not have to be afraid that if he does not blurt it out immediately, the opportunity is forever lost.

If it is truly of God, the Spirit is able to lead with clarity.

UNDERSTAND THAT PUBLIC TONGUES REQUIRE INTERPRETATION

This must be kept plain: if a tongue is given publicly to the church, it should be interpreted.

Paul says:

"Greater is he that prophesieth than he that speaketh with tongues, except he interpret, that the church may receive edifying."

— 1 Corinthians 14:5

The purpose is not merely the utterance itself. The purpose is the profit that comes through interpretation. That is why a person should not be eager merely to give a tongue. He should be concerned that the church be helped.

The tongue is the original utterance given by the Spirit. The interpretation brings the meaning of that utterance into the understanding of the congregation. Both matter. The tongue should not be belittled, and the interpretation should not be neglected.

If there is no interpreter present, then the public tongue should not be given. The person may still speak to himself and to God, but not to the church in that way.

This protects both the speaker and the congregation.

DO NOT USE A TONGUE TO DRAW ATTENTION TO YOURSELF

One of the clearest dangers in public spiritual ministry is self-awareness.

A person may begin in sincerity and yet slip into a desire to be noticed, admired, or recognized. That must be resisted. The purpose of a public tongue is not to demonstrate spirituality. It is not to make a person appear gifted. It is not to establish reputation in the church.

The gifts of the Spirit are tools of love, not trophies of spirituality.

If a person gives a tongue publicly, the focus should remain on what God desires to say, not on the one through whom the utterance comes. Humility protects the purity of the gift.

DO NOT MAKE THE TONGUE EXCESSIVELY LONG

This is a practical point, but it matters.

A public tongue should not become excessive in length, volume, or display. When the utterance becomes unnecessarily prolonged, it may place strain on the service, pressure on the interpreter, and distraction on the people.

This does not mean every tongue must be brief in an unnatural way, but it does mean the speaker should avoid excess. Public utterance in the church is not meant to become performance. Simplicity often helps preserve clarity.

In many cases, those who are mature in these things learn how to give what is needed without unnecessary extension.

BE TEACHABLE

Anyone who may be used in a public tongue must remain teachable.

That means being open to pastoral instruction. It means receiving correction without offense. It means recognizing that sincerity does not place a person beyond accountability.

A person may be genuine and still need help with timing.

He may be sincere and still need help with volume.

He may have a real prompting and still need help understanding when it belongs in the service and when it does not.

If a believer cannot be taught, he is not safe in public ministry.

A Holy Ghost church does not need gifted people only. It needs people who are surrendered, teachable, and willing to be governed by the Word.

RESPECT THE ORDER OF THE HOUSE

Every local church has leadership, and that leadership bears responsibility for the service.

A person giving a public tongue should therefore respect the order of the house. He should not assume that his own sense of leading overrides the pastor, the direction of the service, or the established order of the church.

Spiritual ministry thrives where there is mutual honor.

The one who speaks should honor leadership.

Leadership should honor the Spirit.

The congregation should honor what God is doing.

When those things work together, peace is preserved.

RECOGNIZE THAT NOT EVERY SERVICE IS THE SAME

A believer should also exercise wisdom regarding the setting.

There may be regular worship services where leadership is intentionally making room for a public tongue and interpretation. There may also be settings where the flow of the meeting is different, such as a funeral, a wedding, or a teaching-focused gathering. That does not mean the Spirit is absent, but it may mean that public utterance is not fitting in the same way.

This is why sensitivity matters.

The person who would give a public tongue should not only ask, "Is this real?" but also, "Is this the right setting, the right moment, and the right flow for this expression?"

That kind of wisdom protects the beauty of the gift.

REMEMBER THE GOAL

At the end of all of this, the goal remains the same: edification.

A public tongue is not given to create an unusual moment. It is given so that, through interpretation, the church may receive help from God. If the speaker remembers that, many errors will be avoided.

He will not seek attention.

He will not force the moment.

He will not act carelessly.

He will not resist instruction.

He will simply desire that God be glorified and the people be helped.

That is the right spirit in which to approach a public tongue.

A SACRED RESPONSIBILITY

To give a public tongue in the church is a sacred responsibility.

It is not something to fear, but neither is it something to treat lightly. It should be approached with humility, reverence, peace, faith, and a willingness to submit to scriptural order.

The believer who gives a tongue publicly is not merely acting on an unction alone. He is acting in faith upon the Word of God, yielding to the Spirit so that the congregation may be edified when the interpretation is given.

When believers learn to handle this privilege properly, the church is strengthened. Fear begins to leave. Confidence begins to grow. And the gifts of the Spirit can operate in a way that is pure, orderly, and helpful to the body.

The purpose is edification, not display. Spiritual utterance in the church should be governed by love, humility, faith, and the Word of God.

CHAPTER 28

THINGS TO CONSIDER WHEN INTERPRETING A TONGUE

If a public tongue is a sacred privilege, then interpretation is a sacred responsibility.

The church must never think of interpretation as a small or secondary matter. Interpretation is not merely something added so that a service feels complete. It is the means by which mystery becomes understandable and the church receives profit from what the Spirit has given.

Paul gives us a remarkable sequence when he says:

"How is it then, brethren? when ye come together, every one of you hath a psalm, hath a doctrine, hath a tongue, hath a revelation, hath an interpretation."

— 1 Corinthians 14:26

That verse is extremely important because it shows us that in the gathered church, a tongue and an interpretation are connected with revelation. Paul does not merely say that when the church comes together there may be a tongue and then an explanation. He places revelation in the same flow of the service.

This shows us that what begins as mystery in the Spirit is

meant, in the church, to bring understanding and profit to the people.

That is one reason interpretation must be handled carefully. When tongues and interpretation function rightly in the assembly, the church is not merely experiencing something spiritual. It is receiving light and ministry from the Spirit of God. When churches neglect God's order, they do not merely lose a form of service; they may forfeit revelation God intended to bring to His people.

Paul also says:

"Now, brethren, if I come unto you speaking with tongues, what shall I profit you, except I shall speak to you either by revelation, or by knowledge, or by prophesying, or by doctrine?"

— 1 Corinthians 14:6

This verse tells us what interpreted tongues may become in the church. What begins as tongues does not remain mystery only. When interpreted, it may bring revelation, knowledge, prophesying, or doctrine.

That is a very high standard.

Interpretation is not merely repeating spiritual sound in English. It is bringing forth profit to the church. This is why the one who interprets must be spiritually prepared and scripturally sound. He is not merely filling space after a tongue. He is helping bring understanding, light, and edification to the body of Christ.

With that in mind, anyone who would interpret a public tongue must consider several things.

THE PURPOSE OF INTERPRETATION

The first thing to remember is that interpretation exists for edification.

A tongue spoken publicly without interpretation leaves the church listening to mystery only. But when interpretation is given, the church is brought into understanding. That understanding may come as revelation, knowledge, prophecy, or doctrine, but whatever form it takes, the church should be profited by it.

That is why Paul teaches that a tongue spoken in the church must be interpreted if the church is to receive edifying.

Interpretation is not a performance. It is not an attempt to sound deep, dramatic, or mystical. It is meant to bring profit and help to the body.

INTERPRETATION BRINGS REVELATION AND UNDERSTANDING

This must remain central.

When the church hears a public tongue, it is hearing an utterance given by the Spirit. But when interpretation is given, what was not understood becomes understandable. Light comes. The church receives the meaning of the Spirit-given utterance.

Paul's order in 1 Corinthians 14:26 is not accidental. He speaks of a tongue, a revelation, and an interpretation. That means the church should not look at interpretation as a weak appendix to tongues. It should understand that interpretation is one of God's appointed ways of bringing revelation and understanding into the assembly.

This is why this ministry must never be treated casually.

True revelation in the church will not pull attention away from Christ. And the gifts of the Spirit can operate in a way that is pure, orderly, and bears His character.

Revelation is not merely information. It is disclosure from

heaven. It is the unveiling of what God desires His people to understand.

This agrees with Paul's broader teaching concerning the ministry of the Spirit. He wrote that "the Spirit searcheth all things, yea, the deep things of God," and that God has given us His Spirit "that we might know the things that are freely given to us of God."

— 1 Corinthians 2:10, 12

He then says:

"Which things also we speak, not in the words which man's wisdom teacheth, but which the Holy Ghost teacheth..."

— 1 Corinthians 2:13

This passage is not limited to tongues and interpretation, but it shows the principle by which revelation comes. The Spirit knows the deep things of God, reveals what man could not know naturally, and enables spiritual things to be spoken. That is why interpretation must remain spiritual, scriptural, and Christ-honoring. We are not dealing with human cleverness. We are dealing with things made known by the Spirit of God.

BE SCRIPTURALLY GROUNDED

Paul said:

"Now, brethren, if I come unto you speaking with tongues, what shall I profit you, except I shall speak to you either by revelation, or by knowledge, or by prophesying, or by doctrine?"

— 1 Corinthians 14:6

Paul names four ways spiritual utterance may bring profit to the church:

- Revelation
- Knowledge

- Prophesying
- Doctrine

Because interpretation may bring revelation, knowledge, prophecy, or doctrine, the one who interprets must be scripturally grounded.

A person may have faith and boldness to give a public tongue, but interpretation requires maturity, preparation, scriptural understanding, and sensitivity to the Holy Ghost.

If what is interpreted may bring doctrine, it cannot be careless. If it may bring revelation, it must be true revelation and not imagination. If it may function like prophecy, it must carry the spiritual quality of edification, exhortation, and comfort. If it may bring knowledge, it must agree with the written Word and the character of God.

This is one of the most important practical considerations in the whole matter. Interpretation is too weighty to be handled merely by excitement. It should come through a prepared vessel.

This is also why, in many churches, the pastor is often the most likely to interpret. He is usually the one most grounded in Scripture, most aware of the flow of the service, and most likely to be received by the people.

That does not mean he must always interpret, nor that no one else can. But it does mean interpretation should not be treated as though anyone with enthusiasm is automatically equipped for it.

These are supernatural gifts, but they still flow through prepared vessels. A person's background knowledge, experience, scriptural understanding, and spiritual maturity will affect the clarity and quality of what comes forth.

DO NOT TREAT INTERPRETATION AS TRANSLATION

Interpretation is not necessarily a word-for-word translation.

That must be understood by the church and by the interpreter. The goal is not to match syllables, length, or structure. The goal is to bring forth the sense and substance of what the Spirit is saying so that the church may receive the profit of it.

One tongue may be brief and the interpretation somewhat fuller. Another tongue may be longer and the interpretation more concise. The issue is not mechanical equality. The issue is whether the interpretation truly brings forth what the Spirit intended for the church.

That said, interpretation must not become an excuse for adding what was never given. The interpreter is not free to take a spiritual moment and fill it with personal thoughts. He is not called to improve on the tongue, decorate the tongue, or preach his own sermon under the cover of interpretation.

He is called to yield to the Spirit and bring forth faithfully what the church needs to hear.

Some have asked, "How do you know the interpretation is correct?" It must meet the biblical requirements for spiritual utterance. Yet interpretation does not merely proceed from the mind; it originates with the Holy Ghost and is witnessed in the heart. Therefore, it can be given with humility and boldness.

REMAIN HUMBLE AND TEACHABLE

Anyone who interprets must remain humble.

A person may genuinely be used by God in interpretation and still need correction in wording, tone, timing, or content.

He may mean well and still miss something. He may be sincere and still need pastoral guidance.

Interpretation is too important to be handled by people who cannot receive instruction.

A teachable interpreter is a safe interpreter.

He will not assume every impression is infallible. He will not become defensive if leadership asks questions or brings correction. He will not insist on proving himself. He will want the church helped more than he wants himself vindicated.

This is especially important because interpretation touches revelation. If people become proud in this area, the whole atmosphere of the service may be damaged.

Humility preserves purity.

STAY WITHIN THE CHARACTER OF SIMPLE PROPHECY

Although interpretation is its own gift, in its effect upon the church it functions much like prophecy.

Paul says:

"But he that prophesieth speaketh unto men to edification, and exhortation, and comfort."

— 1 Corinthians 14:3

That does not mean every interpretation will sound mild, but it does mean the overall quality should be spiritually sound, edifying, strengthening, and in keeping with God's nature.

Interpretation should not be used to embarrass people, humiliate people, express private opinions, or pronounce unscriptural judgments in a dramatic tone. The Spirit of God does not need fleshly harshness to make Himself heard.

A good interpreter should therefore ask inwardly:

Does this agree with the Word?

Does this bear the character of God?

Does this carry the spiritual quality of edification, exhortation, and comfort?

Does this honor Christ?

If not, he should be careful.

BE SENSITIVE TO THE FLOW OF THE SERVICE

Interpretation does not happen in a vacuum. It comes in the context of a gathered service.

The interpreter should be sensitive to the atmosphere of the meeting, the tone of the service, and the direction in which leadership is moving. He should not rush ahead. He should not compete with others. He should not seize the moment as though speed proves spirituality.

If one interpreter is designated for that service, then others who may feel they could interpret should honor the order of the house and remain quiet.

This matters because one of the clearest ways disorder enters is through competing interpretations. One person gives an interpretation, another is dissatisfied and gives a second, and perhaps another tries to improve both. That lowers the standard of the gifts in the eyes of the people. It draws attention away from what God is saying and toward the mechanics of who said what.

Scripture's wisdom is simple: let one interpret.

That protects clarity, peace, and confidence in the service.

DO NOT GO BEYOND WHAT GOD GIVES

The interpreter should also resist the temptation to go beyond what God has given.

Sometimes a person may begin accurately and then continue in the flesh. Sometimes he may receive the true essence of the interpretation and then add his own thoughts, warnings, or emphases. That is always dangerous.

The safest course is simplicity, clarity, and restraint.

Say what God is saying.

Do not add what He has not given.

This is one reason maturity matters. Immature people often feel pressure to make the interpretation sound impressive. Mature people are content to be accurate.

LET REVELATION POINT THE CHURCH TO CHRIST

Because interpretation brings understanding and revelation, it must not merely sound spiritual. It must reveal Christ, honor Christ, and agree with Christ.

The church is founded on the revelation of Jesus Christ. Therefore, interpretation that truly comes from the Spirit will not magnify the interpreter, build a personality, or create fascination with the vessel. It will leave the church more aware of the Lord, more conscious of His truth, more established in His Word, and more yielded to His will.

That is one of the best tests of all.

When interpretation is genuine and healthy, Jesus is honored.

RECOGNIZE THE WEIGHT OF THIS MINISTRY

A church that wants steady revelation must also want qualified interpretation.

That is why churches should not leave this area undeveloped. If there is no interpreter, public tongues will eventually be silenced or reduced. If there are careless interpreters, prophecy may be despised and confidence in the gifts may diminish.

But where there is a qualified, scripturally sound, humble, teachable, recognized interpreter, revelation can flow in the church with peace and order.

Paul's pattern is not vague. When the church comes together, a tongue, a revelation, and an interpretation all have a place. And when the tongue is interpreted, what is spoken may bring revelation, knowledge, prophecy, or doctrine for the profit of the church.

That is not confusion.

That is one of God's appointed ways of speaking among His people.

A HOLY RESPONSIBILITY

To interpret a tongue publicly is a holy responsibility.

It is not something to fear if God has equipped and prepared the vessel. But neither is it something to approach lightly. The one who interprets must remember that he is handling spiritual utterance being brought into understanding for the profit of the church.

He must remain yielded to the Spirit, grounded in the Word, submitted to leadership, and aware that the church is receiving more than sound. It is receiving ministry from God.

When interpretation is handled properly, the people are strengthened, the gifts are honored, the service remains in peace and order, and Jesus Christ is exalted. That is what we should desire.

CHAPTER 29

THINGS TO CONSIDER WHEN JUDGING PROPHECY

If prophecy is to have a healthy place in the church, then the church must also understand how prophecy is to be judged.

This is one of the most important practical matters in a Holy Ghost church. Many congregations have gone wrong in one of two directions. Some have accepted nearly every utterance without discernment, as though anything that sounds spiritual must automatically be from God. Others have become so guarded and suspicious that almost nothing is ever allowed to be spoken.

Both extremes are harmful.

The answer is not careless acceptance, and it is not fearful silence. The answer is scriptural judgment.

Paul gives us a clear instruction:

"Let the prophets speak two or three, and let the other judge."

— 1 Corinthians 14:29

That verse alone teaches us several important things.

First, prophecy is to be allowed a place in the church.

Second, it is to be limited and ordered.

Third, it is to be judged.

This means that judging prophecy is not optional. It is part of how a New Testament church protects purity while still making room for the Spirit to move.

PROPHECY MUST BE SPOKEN BEFORE IT CAN BE JUDGED

One of the first things to understand is the order Paul gives.

He does not say, "Judge whether anyone should ever speak." He says, "Let the prophets speak two or three, and let the other judge." Speak first, then judge.

That order matters.

Many churches and leaders have judged prophecy before it was ever given. They became so cautious, so concerned about error, and so afraid of disorder that they effectively removed public utterance altogether. But Paul did not tell the church to prevent all utterance in order to stay safe. He told them to let the prophets speak, and then let the others judge. Speak, then judge.

That is a healthier and more biblical pattern.

If everything is silenced before it is spoken, then the church never develops in discernment. It only develops in fear. But when prophecy is allowed to come forth within scriptural order, mature believers and leaders may then weigh what has been said.

This is important because some churches have no prophecy at all, not because God is unwilling to speak, but because the people have judged everything prematurely. They have shut the door before the utterance ever had a chance to come forth.

A Holy Ghost church must not do that. A Holy Ghost church will not do that.

JUDGMENT IS NOT REJECTION

To judge prophecy is not to despise prophecy. Keep in mind, it is the utterance that is being judged, not the person giving the utterance. Some believers hear the word "judge" and immediately think of harsh criticism, embarrassment, or public rejection. That is not Paul's meaning. To judge prophecy is to weigh it, test it, and discern it properly. It is to ask whether what has been spoken truly agrees with the Word of God, the Spirit of God, and the character of God. When done rightly, judgment does not quench the Spirit; it protects the church and preserves the purity of what the Spirit is saying.

Paul gives another balanced instruction in 1 Thessalonians:

"Quench not the Spirit.

Despise not prophesyings.

Prove all things; hold fast that which is good."

— 1 Thessalonians 5:19–21

In other words, do not shut everything down, do not treat prophecy with contempt, but do test and weigh what is spoken. Then hold fast that which is good.

That is the balance the church must keep.

We are not to quench the Spirit, and we are not to despise prophesyings. We are told to prove all things and hold fast that which is good.

This kind of judgment is necessary because not everything that sounds spiritual should be accepted as though it came from God. A person may be sincere and still mix in the flesh. A person may mean well and still speak beyond what God actually gave. A person may have a genuine prompting and yet express it imperfectly.

That is why mature judgment is needed.

Judgment protects the church without silencing the Spirit.

Judgment preserves purity without producing fear.

Judgment helps the people receive what is true and set aside what is not.

THIS ESPECIALLY CONCERNS MATURE LEADERS

In the context of 1 Corinthians 14, this judging is not placed primarily into the hands of the whole congregation in a loose and careless way. It especially concerns those who are spiritually mature and qualified to discern what is being spoken.

Paul says, "Let the prophets speak two or three, and let the other judge" (1 Corinthians 14:29). The context suggests recognized spiritual people in the assembly, not a room full of untrained reactions.

This is one of the reasons leadership matters so much in a Holy Ghost church. Leaders help the church discern without crushing. They help maintain standards without removing liberty. They help weigh what is spoken in a way that protects peace.

This keeps judging prophecy from turning into a public spectacle. The point is not that everyone in the room should immediately announce his opinion. The point is that mature, spiritual people must weigh what has been said and recognize whether it is sound.

JUDGE BY THE WORD OF GOD

The first and greatest standard for judging prophecy is the written Word of God.

God will not speak in prophecy contrary to what He has already spoken in Scripture. He will not inspire something that denies His nature, contradicts His truth, or opposes the gospel of Jesus Christ.

That means prophecy must never be judged merely by how powerful it sounded, how emotional it felt, or how impressed people were by the delivery. The standard is higher than that.

Does it agree with the Word?

Does it honor Christ?

Does it reflect the character of God?

Does it remain within the boundaries of New Testament truth?

If not, it is not to be received simply because it was spoken with intensity.

This is one reason mature churches place such value on biblical teaching. The stronger a church is in the Word, the better equipped it will be to judge prophecy rightly.

JUDGE BY THE CHARACTER OF GOD

Prophecy must also be judged by the character of God.

God is not the author of confusion, but of peace. He is holy, truthful, wise, and loving. He may correct, but even His correction is pure. He may warn, but His warnings do not contradict His own nature.

This matters because people sometimes excuse harsh, fleshly, or manipulative utterances by saying, "God was really moving." But if the tone, spirit, or effect of what was spoken is unlike the character of God, then it should be weighed very carefully.

God does not need fleshly drama to make Himself known.

He does not need confusion to demonstrate power.

He does not need manipulation to speak to His people.

The Spirit of God moves in peace.

JUDGE BY THE FRUIT OF SIMPLE PROPHECY

Paul gives us another important measure when he says:

"But he that prophesieth speaketh unto men to edification, and exhortation, and comfort."

— 1 Corinthians 14:3

The general quality of prophecy in the church should edify, exhort, strengthen, and comfort the people. It should not produce fear, humiliation, confusion, or spiritual oppression.

When prophecy is judged, three important questions should be asked:

- Did it edify?
- Did it exhort?
- Did it comfort?

A true word may challenge people, but even then it should carry the witness of the Holy Ghost, not the pressure of human opinion or emotion.

This protects the church from dramatic utterances that may sound powerful but leave the people unsettled in the wrong way.

DO NOT CONFUSE INSPIRATION WITH INFALLIBILITY

A person may be genuinely inspired and still not be infallible in delivery.

That is something every Holy Ghost church must remember.

God may truly move on a person, and yet that person may add something unnecessary, speak with poor timing, choose weak wording, or mix human emotion into what should have remained simple and pure.

That does not mean the whole thing was false. It means prophecy must be judged wisely.

This helps churches stay balanced. We do not need to act as though every imperfection makes an utterance worthless. Neither do we need to act as though a genuine beginning makes everything that followed untouchable.

Mature judgment can recognize what is of God and what may have been added by man.

This is one reason humility must remain central for those who speak.

PUBLIC JUDGMENT MUST NOT BECOME PUBLIC HUMILIATION

There is also wisdom needed in how prophecy is judged.

Not every matter must be handled in a public, dramatic way. Leadership should use wisdom. Some correction may need to happen privately. Some instruction may be given later through teaching. Some issues may need direct pastoral response in the moment. But in all of this, the purpose is not humiliation. It is protection, instruction, and peace.

A church should not create an atmosphere where people are terrified to yield because they fear being publicly embarrassed. Neither should it create an atmosphere where no one is ever corrected.

Again, balance is needed.

A wise pastor knows how to honor the Holy Ghost and protect the people.

MOVED BY THE SPIRIT, YET STILL RESPONSIBLE

Paul continues:

"If any thing be revealed to another that sitteth by, let the first hold his peace.

For ye may all prophesy one by one, that all may learn, and all may be comforted.

And the spirits of the prophets are subject to the prophets."

— 1 Corinthians 14:30–32

These verses remind us that people who prophesy are not out of control. They are still responsible for how they yield. They can wait. They can stop. They can defer. They can speak one by one.

This is important in judging prophecy because sometimes people excuse disorder by claiming they could not help themselves. Paul removes that excuse. The spirit of the prophet is subject to the prophet.

That means timing matters.

Tone matters.

Self-control matters.

Submission to order matters.

When prophecy is judged, both the content and the manner in which it was brought forth may need to be weighed. Was it given in peace? Was it properly timed? Was it submitted to the order of the service? These things matter because God is not the author of confusion.

GOD IS NOT THE AUTHOR OF CONFUSION

Paul closes this section by saying:

"For God is not the author of confusion, but of peace, as in all churches of the saints."

— 1 Corinthians 14:33

This statement governs the judging of prophecy just as much as it governs the giving of prophecy.

If the result of an utterance is rivalry, disorder, uncertainty, or pressure, something is wrong. God's work in the church is not advanced by confusion. His voice may be strong, but it is not chaotic. His presence may be powerful, but it does not destroy peace.

That means the judging of prophecy should aim at peace, not by avoiding the truth, but by handling the truth with wisdom, love, and order.

THE GOAL IS THAT ALL MAY LEARN

Paul says that when these things function rightly, "all may learn, and all may be comforted" (1 Corinthians 14:31).

That is the goal.

Judging prophecy is not meant to choke the service. It is meant to help the church learn. The prophets learn. The leaders learn. The congregation learns. And the church is comforted because the gifts are no longer operating in fear or confusion, but in clarity and peace.

A healthy church does not fear judgment. It values it, because where prophecy is judged rightly, the genuine is protected, the flesh is exposed, and the people gain confidence that what is happening among them is sound.

A HOLY RESPONSIBILITY

To judge prophecy is a holy responsibility.

It must not be done carelessly, harshly, or proudly. It must be done with discernment, humility, scriptural grounding, and pastoral wisdom.

The church that refuses to judge prophecy becomes vulnerable to confusion. When a church tries to judge everything before it is spoken, the result is not a Holy Ghost-inspired utterance, but no utterance at all. Over-control does not produce a better manifestation; it can silence the manifestation altogether.

But the church that follows Paul's order, letting prophets speak and then judging what is spoken, can enjoy both liberty and safety.

When prophecy is judged properly, the Church is protected, the people are instructed, and the Spirit is not quenched. Prophecy is given room, but it is not left without order. Spiritual utterance ought to be kept in line with God's Word, God's peace, and God's purpose for the church.

CHAPTER 30

WHY A HOLY GHOST CHURCH IS BOTH REASONABLE AND NECESSARY

By this point in our study, some may still ask a sincere question:

Is all of this really necessary?

Is it necessary to make room for spiritual utterance in the church?

Is it necessary to teach on tongues, interpretation, prophecy, and order?

Is it necessary to seek to become not only a Word church, but a Holy Ghost church?

The answer is yes.

And it is not only necessary; it is reasonable.

These gifts are reasonable and necessary. Some people hear the phrase "Holy Ghost church" and immediately think of excess, emotionalism, or unusual behavior. Others think of something unpredictable, difficult to explain, and perhaps unnecessary in a modern church setting.

Judging by Scripture, a Holy Ghost church is not unreasonable. It should not seem strange at all, because it is simply a church that makes room for what God Himself placed in the Church.

IT IS REASONABLE BECAUSE GOD GAVE THE SPIRIT TO THE CHURCH

The Holy Spirit was not given as an ornament. He was not poured out merely to create a moment in history. He was given to abide with the believer and to work in the Church.

Jesus said:

"And I will pray the Father, and he shall give you another Comforter, that he may abide with you for ever."

—John 14:16

The Spirit was given because the Church needs Him. It is not extreme for a church to welcome Him, make room for Him, and desire His manifestations. What would be unreasonable is to claim that God gave the Spirit to the Church, yet expect the Church to function as though His present ministry were not needed.

IT IS REASONABLE BECAUSE THE NEW TESTAMENT DESCRIBES IT

A Holy Ghost church is reasonable because it is biblical.

We are not trying to invent some new model. We are not trying to create a strange or novel expression of Christianity. We are simply looking at the New Testament and taking seriously what it describes.

Paul said that when the church comes together there is a psalm, a doctrine, a tongue, a revelation, and an interpretation. He told us not to be ignorant concerning spiritual things. He told us to desire spiritual gifts, not to forbid speaking with tongues, and to let all things be done unto edifying, decently, and in order.

None of that is unreasonable.

It only seems unreasonable if we have decided in advance that church should be shaped more by modern comfort, human predictability, or religious tradition than by apostolic instruction.

IT IS REASONABLE BECAUSE THE CHURCH IS BUILT ON REVELATION

The Church is not built merely on information. It is built on revelation.

Peter said:

"Thou art the Christ, the Son of the living God."

— Matthew 16:16

And Jesus answered:

"...flesh and blood hath not revealed it unto thee, but my Father which is in heaven... upon this rock I will build my church..."

— Matthew 16:17–18

The Church of Jesus Christ is founded upon heaven-given revelation concerning the person of Christ, and true prophecy will always bear witness to Him. This is why a Holy Ghost church is reasonable and necessary. It is a church that recognizes that God still works by His Spirit in ways that agree with His written Word and reveal Christ to His people. We are not talking about adding to Scripture. We are talking about the Spirit of God making truth living, present, and powerful in the midst of the assembly.

A church that makes room for revelation is not abandoning reason. It is honoring the very foundation on which the Church is built.

IT IS REASONABLE BECAUSE THE GIFTS WERE GIVEN TO HELP PEOPLE

The gifts of the Spirit were given to profit the Church, they were given to bless and help the body of Christ.

Words of wisdom and knowledge, prophecy, tongues and interpretation, discerning of spirits, special faith, healings, and miracles all help the Church. They are tools of love in the hands of believers to bless and edify the Church.

If a church believes that people still need strength, direction, comfort, correction, healing, encouragement, and spiritual help, then it is only reasonable that the church should welcome the means by which God has provided for those needs.

What is unreasonable is to admit the needs remain while acting as though God's provision is no longer necessary.

IT IS NECESSARY BECAUSE THE CHURCH TENDS TO DRIFT

A Holy Ghost church is not only reasonable. It is necessary because churches tend to drift.

They drift into empty routine.

They drift into structure without life.

They drift into preaching without manifestation.

They drift into familiarity without expectancy.

That drift is always a danger.

This is why a Holy Ghost church must be intentional.

Without teaching, expectation, and room for the Spirit to move, many churches slowly become functional but spiritually thin, orderly but lacking in fullness, biblical in content but limited in manifestation. Scripture warns, "The man that wandereth out of the way of understanding shall remain in the congregation of the dead" (Proverbs 21:16). When a church wanders from what the Word says about the ministry of the Spirit, it may retain the form while losing the power. Paul warned of "a form of godliness, but denying the power thereof" (2 Timothy 3:5).

They need the strengthening, comforting, correcting, and revealing ministry of the Holy Ghost. They need the anointing of the Holy Ghost, because only the Spirit can make ministry more than words and church life more than religious routine. Christianity is not merely something to study; it is a life to be lived in the presence and power of God.

Religious form may train the mind while leaving the heart untouched. But where the Word is honored and the Spirit is welcomed, people are not only informed; they are quickened, anointed, and changed.

IT IS NECESSARY BECAUSE THE WORLD NEEDS A SPIRIT-EMPOWERED CHURCH

The world needs more than religion. It needs a Church filled with the Holy Ghost, anointed by God, and moving in the power of the Spirit. Paul described such a gathering:

"And thus are the secrets of his heart made manifest; and so falling down on his face he will worship God, and report that God is in you of a truth."

— 1 Corinthians 14:25

Unbelievers may not understand tongues. They may not

understand prophecy. They may not understand the atmosphere of a Spirit-filled service. But when the Holy Ghost is truly moving, they know that they have encountered something real.

That is not fanatical.

That is biblical.

That is what happens when God is given room to work among His people.

A Holy Ghost church is therefore necessary not only for believers, but also for the witness of the Church before the world.

IT IS NECESSARY BECAUSE THE LAST DAYS REQUIRE SPIRITUAL STRENGTH

We are not living in a light hour. We are living in serious times.

Believers need strength.

Pastors need wisdom.

Churches need discernment.

Families need help.

Congregations need more than polished services and predictable routines.

The Church needs the Holy Ghost.

We need His comfort.

We need His direction.

We need His power.

We need His revelation.

We need His utterance.

We need His help in prayer and intercession.

To say this is necessary is not to diminish the Word. It is to obey the Word. The Scriptures themselves direct us to desire spiritual gifts, to pray in the Spirit, to welcome the Spirit's ministry, and to let all things be done in order.

IT IS REASONABLE AND NECESSARY TO RETURN TO THE PATTERN

A Holy Ghost church is not an oddity. It is not an exaggerated version of church life. It is a return to the New Testament pattern.

It is reasonable because it follows Scripture. It is necessary because the Church still needs what God gave. The Holy Ghost was not given for the first generation only. He was given to abide with us. Revelation is still foundational. The gifts of the Spirit still edify. The power of God is still needed. People still need more than religious form.

The question is not whether men can build something that appears successful. The question is whether we will be satisfied with less than the pattern God gave us in His Word.

A church can have order and still have life. It can have structure and still have the Spirit. It can honor the Word and still make room for the Holy Ghost.

THE KIND OF CHURCH WE SHOULD DESIRE

We should desire a church where the Word is honored, the Spirit is welcomed, love governs, and order protects liberty; a church where revelation flows, prophecy is weighed, tongues are interpreted, and Jesus is glorified.

Such a church is not beyond reach. It is not reserved for another generation or a select few. It is the church Paul described, the church Scripture permits, and the church the Holy Ghost still desires.

The exhortation stands before us: make your church not only a Word church, but a Holy Ghost church. It is a call from God, and the most reasonable and necessary response is simply, Yes, Lord.

May our answer be yes.

APPENDIX A
HOW TO BE SAVED

The most important thing that can ever happen in a person's life is to receive Jesus Christ as Lord and Savior and be born again. Nothing is more important, because salvation determines a person's eternal destiny.

Jesus said:

"Except a man be born again, he cannot see the kingdom of God."

—John 3:3

To be born again means to receive new life from God. Salvation is not merely joining a church, turning over a new leaf, or trying to become a better person. Salvation comes through Jesus Christ, who died for our sins, rose again from the dead, and offers eternal life to all who believe on Him.

The Bible tells us why salvation is necessary:

"For all have sinned, and come short of the glory of God."

— Romans 3:23

Sin has separated man from God, and no person can save

himself by good works, religious effort, or personal merit. But God loved us and sent His Son to die for us.

"But God commendeth his love toward us, in that, while we were yet sinners, Christ died for us."

— Romans 5:8

Jesus took our place. He bore our sins. He shed His blood for our redemption. Through His death, burial, and resurrection, salvation is available to all who receive Him.

"But as many as received him, to them gave he power to become the sons of God, even to them that believe on his name:"

— John 1:12

The Bible says:

"Repent ye therefore, and be converted, that your sins may be blotted out..."

— Acts 3:19

And again:

"For whosoever shall call upon the name of the Lord shall be saved."

— Romans 10:13

Salvation is received by faith. A person must repent of sin, believe in the Lord Jesus Christ, and confess Him as Lord.

"That if thou shalt confess with thy mouth the Lord Jesus, and shalt believe in thine heart that God hath raised him from the dead, thou shalt be saved.

For with the heart man believeth unto righteousness; and with the mouth confession is made unto salvation."

— Romans 10:9–10

Dear one, you can be saved right now. Turn from your sins and believe that Jesus Christ is the Son of God, that He died for you, and that God raised Him from the dead. Receive Him now as your Lord and Savior.

PRAYER TO RECEIVE JESUS CHRIST

Lord God, I come to You in the Name of Jesus.

I know that I am a sinner. I know that without You I am lost.

I believe that Jesus Christ is the Son of God. I believe He died for my sins and that You raised Him from the dead.

I repent of my sins, and I turn to You now.

Lord Jesus, come into my heart and life. Save me now. Wash me clean. Make me a new creature in Christ.

I confess Jesus Christ as my Lord and Savior.

Thank You, Lord, for saving me now.

In Jesus' Name, Amen.

If you prayed this sincerely from your heart, according to the Word of God, you are now a saved child of God, and you have a home in heaven. You have called upon the Name of the Lord, and the Bible says:

"For whosoever shall call upon the name of the Lord shall be saved."

— Romans 10:13

Begin to read the Bible daily, pray and talk to God, and become part of a Bible-believing church where Jesus is honored, the Word of God is taught, and the Holy Ghost is welcomed.

APPENDIX B

HOW TO BE FILLED WITH THE HOLY GHOST

After receiving Jesus Christ as Lord and Savior, the next step is to be filled with the Holy Ghost. A person must first be a born-again child of God in order to receive this Holy Ghost baptism. Salvation is necessary for eternal life and a new life in Christ. The baptism with the Holy Ghost is God's promise to every believer, and it is necessary. You need power to live this Christian life.

When Paul met certain disciples at Ephesus, he asked them:

"Have ye received the Holy Ghost since ye believed?"

— Acts 19:2

This question shows us that believing comes first, and receiving the Holy Ghost follows as a promise made available to believers. Salvation brings us into Christ. The baptism with the Holy Ghost clothes us with power from on high.

Jesus said:

"If ye then, being evil, know how to give good gifts unto your children: how much more shall your heavenly Father give the Holy Spirit to them that ask him?"

— Luke 11:13

God is not reluctant to fill His children with the Holy Ghost. He is a good Father. If you are saved, you may come to Him with confidence and ask to be filled with the Spirit.

A believer may receive while another Spirit-filled believer lays hands on him and prays. This is biblical. Paul laid hands on the believers at Ephesus, and Scripture says:

"And when Paul had laid his hands upon them, the Holy Ghost came on them; and they spake with tongues, and prophesied."

— Acts 19:6

A believer may also ask God directly and receive by faith. The power is not in man's hands. The Father gives the Holy Spirit to them that ask Him.

The Bible says:

"And this is the confidence that we have in him, that, if we ask any thing according to his will, he heareth us:

And if we know that he hear us, whatsoever we ask, we know that we have the petitions that we desired of him."

— 1 John 5:14–15

Since the baptism with the Holy Ghost is the will of God for believers, you can ask in faith, knowing that He hears you and grants what you have asked according to His Word.

When you receive the Holy Ghost, you should expect to speak with other tongues as the Spirit gives utterance. On the Day of Pentecost, the Bible says:

"And they were all filled with the Holy Ghost, and began to speak with other tongues, as the Spirit gave them utterance."

— Acts 2:4

Notice the order. They were filled with the Holy Ghost, and they began to speak. The Spirit gave the utterance, but they did the speaking.

The Holy Ghost will not force you to speak. He will not take control of your mouth against your will. You must yield to Him and cooperate with Him. Open your mouth, lift your voice, move your tongue and lips, and begin to speak the words and syllables that come from your spirit by the Holy Ghost.

Do not wait for the Spirit to make you speak. He gives the utterance, but you speak. Do not try to form words with your natural mind. Tongues do not come from the understanding. They come from your spirit by the help of the Holy Ghost.

Paul said:

"For if I pray in an unknown tongue, my spirit prayeth, but my understanding is unfruitful."

— 1 Corinthians 14:14

When you pray in tongues, your spirit is praying. Your understanding may not know what is being said, but your spirit is speaking by the help of the Holy Ghost.

PRAYER TO BE FILLED WITH THE HOLY GHOST

Dear Lord Jesus, I thank You that I am Your child. You are my Lord, and I believe that God raised You from the dead.

As Your child, I ask You now to fill me with the gift of the Holy Ghost.

I receive the Holy Ghost now by faith. I believe I receive what You promised. I expect to speak with other tongues as the Spirit gives me utterance.

Thank You, Lord, for saving me. Thank You for filling me now with Your precious Holy Spirit.

I receive Him by faith, and I yield myself to Him now.

In Jesus' Name, Amen.

After you pray this prayer, lift your voice and begin to speak.

Do not speak in your known language, and do not wait for God to force you. Yield to the Holy Ghost and speak the words and syllables that rise from within.

You may only speak a few words at first. That is all right. Continue to yield. Continue to speak. Continue to pray in the Spirit. As you do, you will grow more confident and more familiar with the flow of the Holy Ghost.

Speaking with tongues is the initial evidence of being filled with the Holy Ghost, but it is also more than an initial sign. It opens the door to a life of praying in the Spirit, worshiping God beyond the limits of natural speech, and becoming more sensitive to the things of the Spirit.

The baptism with the Holy Ghost is a precious gift. Receive by faith, yield to the Spirit, and continue to pray in tongues as part of your Spirit-filled life.

ABOUT THE AUTHOR

Gary B. Bailey has preached and taught the gospel of Jesus Christ for nearly fifty years, carrying a message of faith in God and ministry in the Spirit. In his early ministry, while ministering on the Navajo Nation, the Lord spoke Zechariah 8:9 to his heart: "Let your hands be strong." From that scripture, Brother Gary received a directive to strengthen the hands of believers and encourage them to get about the work of the ministry.

That same charge is reflected in this book. With a balanced approach to the Word of God and the ministry of the Holy Ghost, Brother Gary writes to encourage pastors, leaders, and churches to recover a New Testament pattern: the Word preached with power, the Spirit welcomed, the gifts of the Spirit given room to operate, and Jesus glorified.

~